T0115047

Primary Gift

Awaken to the Excellence of
Your Life's Journey

Kelly F. Holland

BALBOA.
PRESS
A DIVISION OF HAY HOUSE

Balboa Press books may be ordered through booksellers or by contacting:

Balboa Press
A Division of Hay House
1663 Liberty Drive
Bloomington, IN 47403
www.balboapress.com
1 (877) 407-4847

Printed in the United States of America.

ISBN: 978-1-4525-9416-3 (sc)
ISBN: 978-1-4525-9417-0 (hc)
ISBN: 978-1-4525-9415-6 (e)

Library of Congress Control Number: 2014904569

Balboa Press rev. date: 05/14/2014

This book is dedicated to all the people who live with unparalleled desire, passion, and electricity to light up the world. This book is for all those in search of hope, inspiration, and world-class excellence in all of life's offerings.

People like us allow each of us to tell our stories so that we may provide the evidence that life's dreams really can come true and ensure everyone that the universe really provides a lighted, guided path so that we may discover and unfold the primary gifts of our lives.

Acknowledgments

My journey has been amazing, and I want to thank my family, friends, employers, co-workers, counselors and teachers, and divine pets for everything you have given me. This book is an expression of the love and appreciation I hold for each and every one of you. For it is greatly known that in the success of one person, there are many who have supported that process.

To my mother; you have been my teacher, my student, and my life's best friend. Thank you for the journey that we have walked together and for the gift that has become my life. The genius that I have discovered in myself is merely a reflection of the genius that lives within you.

To my psychologist, Denise L. Gulledge, PhD; thank you for all that you have given me in my life, my heart, and my person. The teacher I have found in you and the love and guidance that you have provided have made this book possible. Your grace, your love, your teachings, and your wisdom have helped guide and shape me personally, professionally, and spiritually. My life is a reflection of your influence.

To my maternal grandparents; from my earliest years, your love and dedication to my siblings and me was the difference in our lives. And as we grew, your love for us never changed. Thank you for your love and tireless work to provide for your family. It is what allowed each one of us to live a quality of life that we otherwise would not have known. Thank you for your standards that live within me today!

To my uncle and two aunts; you have stood beside me for decades with unrelenting love and dedication to my overall success in life. Thank you for believing in me and for showing me how acts of generosity can never be measured by the dollar amount given but in the dream that was allowed to unfold.

To my siblings; you are my heart and soul in life. What you experienced, I experienced. We are connected—and we are one. Thank you for allowing me the freedom to journey through life as your younger sister.

And finally, to my literary midwife, Sherry Folb; thank you for your talent, your wisdom, and your gentle, kind heart as you took me under your wing and guided me through the process of writing my first book. I appreciate and respect your devotion to our work and your desire to bring out my best. You have touched my life.

Contents

Awaken to the Excellence of Your Life's Journey

To awaken to the excellence of your life's journey is to allow
appreciation to find your heart—for all that you have seen,
for all that you have lived, for all persons you have known. It
is to allow humility to find your character—to embrace rather
than to resist, to love rather than to judge, and to respect
rather than to disdain the teacher in all human diversity.
To awaken to the excellence of your life's journey is to trust that the
process of life is leading to your greatest knowing—of love, appreciation,
and wisdom. It is to discover the joy in the life you came here to live.
To awaken to the excellence of your life's journey
is to receive life's primary gift.

Excellence

From life, I have learned of its presence.
From life, I have learned of its standard.
From life, I have learned of it in all of life's teachings.
From life, I have learned to treasure all that is excellent.
Today, I am able to see, feel, and know the
excellence that exists in all that is.
Today, I am beginning to live the excellence
that has always lived within me.

Inspiration

To stand and to be called.
To stand and to call.
From life, I know inspiration.
It is a gift from the heart.
It is a gift for the heart.
To be on fire for your life is the greatest gift of all.

Introduction

Today I know of excellence.
It is my vision.
It is what lives in my heart.
Today, excellence is my message.

Today I know of inspiration.
It is my vision.
It is what lives within my heart.
Today, inspiration is my message.

———————✦———————

I've wanted to write a book for many years and share my heart, my passion and profound appreciation and wisdom that have come forth from my life's journey. My hope and prayer for this book is that I may inspire you to know that no matter where you start in life – no matter what your circumstances may be – a life that you can dream, you can live fully. To begin, you must release all negative thoughts and beliefs about your life and trust that there is perfection in your journey. The key is to allow appreciation to find your heart for all that you have lived, so love and joy and your inner genius can, powerfully, guide your life.

For fifty years and beyond, I have been a student in life. Today, I have become a teacher. I've had many powerful teachers, and I have learned much from them. Perhaps the most challenging aspect I've encountered has been the knowledge and awareness that wisdom has always lived deeply within me, evolving and maturing. Yet, until recently, I've not been able to express that wisdom for others to see or know.

With love and humility, I have discovered my life's primary gift and the excellence of my life's journey. Today, I am able to share with you the wisdom that has become my own so that in some way, you may also discover your life's primary gift and the excellence of your life's journey.

In the beginning, my wisdom taught me respect for mental and physical illness and the many types of schools in life, with varying degrees of intensity. Those schools can be about life struggles and hardships or about performing and showing the world what is possible to embody. Those schools can be about becoming a teacher and sharing your wisdom or about discovering the universe and unconditional love.

With maturity, my wisdom taught me how to move away from circumstances or events that kept me from living my best life and kept me from hearing and feeling the love of my inner being and the love of others. I was guided toward opportunities that provided positive growth and redirection for my life. I was guided toward discovering my life's purpose.

I learned how to focus, how to sharpen my saw, and how to carve out everything that my wisdom has inspired. I was led to discover my life's heroes. Through them, I discovered my life's dreams. It was then that my heart came to life. I found passion for living. I learned how to allow my dreams to unfold at just the right time. Ultimately, my wisdom taught me great respect for the perfection of my life's journey.

When I think back about my life, excellence and inspiration now live within my heart. I often ask myself, "How could this be, with the life that I have lived, to have come out on the other side of this journey feeling so inspired? What is the meaning?" I believe that no matter what circumstances you may find yourself in, excellence is present. And, no matter how desolate you may feel, when you find the fire, the inspiration, and the music of your heart, there isn't anything that can keep you from living your dreams.

Life is about empowerment, appreciation, and passion. It is also about the electricity that can light up the world, a work ethic and desire for excellence, and communication and co-creation with the universe. It is experiencing how one person can mean the world to another. It only takes one loving, wise heart to make a difference.

Life allows us to learn that when you are in need of something, whether it be love, discipline, boundaries, or a loving relationship, and you give these things to another, you are giving to yourself as well. It is to know that life can be full of love that is so rich and encompassing that it becomes the foundation for your entire life—the 'soil' from all that you create. It is to understand that pure, unconditional love is the greatest nutrition for your mind, body and spirit and provides you with your greatest resource to create a life worth living.

I ask myself, "Who am I to think that I can somehow make a difference in this world?" But then I remember the passion that lives within my heart and the fire that has erupted in me from the role models who have blessed me with their presences. How could something this powerful not be of benefit for those who will listen? My life has known great struggle, and I have come out standing tall on the other side. Today, I am empowered by all that I have lived.

My prayer is to inspire the youth of the world to recognize the opportunities that lie before you. What an exciting time to have your life ahead of you! There is so much to choose from in our world, but there are many responsibilities that come from these life choices. Your life experiences may be heavy with burden or easy and fun; the life that you ultimately live will depend on the choices that you make. There is not a bad choice. All choices lead to outcomes. What outcomes do you want for your life?

The struggles that you may have witnessed from previous generations are not yours to live. Your life is meant to be different. Allow the decisions of those who came before you to help you make decisions that will lead you to live a life of greater ease and quicker, greater success. Allow your focus to stay positive, and your life will be positive. Seek out the company of others who allow you to walk the earth a better person, personally and professionally. Seek out those persons in life who allow your heart to sing in all that you do and in all that you live.

You are a generation of modern technology, creativity, and invention. Your brains are wired specifically for your lifetime, and you have the opportunity to lead mankind in a new direction where the power and focus of your mind is your greatest tool. The pace of creation is very fast, just as fast as our thoughts. Technology allows rapid returns, and the resources of our world are closer than at any time in history. Reach out and access what you now have available to you. The life that you wish to live is there for you. Choose it! Go get it! Live your inspirations! Discover the leader who lives within you, and allow your greatness to shine brightly for others to see and to know. Mostly, embody the courage to live a life that shows others what is possible. Our world needs you.

Today I understand that no matter what our circumstances may be or the struggles that we may encounter, any life is possible. Today, I cherish the opportunity to live my life. I appreciate my place on earth and my life's experiences. I respect what I have been given in family, friends, and my professional career. When I was young, my vision was limited. There was much that stood in front of the life I wanted to live. At the same time, I could feel the light of life within me. I searched the universe to find my answers. Today, I can see fully and clearly how to live my best life. It is a vision that lives within my mind and a passion that I can feel in my heart. I wish the same for you.

May my story be served as an inspiration for what is possible in any person's life—with a little determination, a ton of passion, and a belief that you can create anything you can imagine. I hope it demonstrates that the quality of one's life is not determined by what you have been given but rather by what you do with what you have been given. It is not where you start. It's where you are headed that matters most.

Chapter 1

Pilot House—A Sanctuary for Adolescents

Seeing Goodness in All Things: That's the God within Us

From an early age, I understood that the fear and despair that was so prevalent in my physical world would not inform the person I came here to be. Today, I am aware that my mother was not the person she came here to be but was merely a character in my play so that I could learn some of the greatest lessons in life, such as humility, appreciation, respect, and perseverance.

As I see the world through the eyes of God, I understand the greatness of my life's journey, and I appreciate the parents that I was given. To see the world through the eyes of God is to see the goodness in all things.

I was born to a mother who had schizophrenia and a father who was an alcoholic. He was absent all of my life. Due to the severity of my mom's mental illness, my maternal grandparents and my two aunts played a large role in helping my mom raise my siblings and me.

When I was about two years old, I knew that I was my mother's teacher and her guardian. I also knew that our relationship was unlike her relationship with my siblings. When I talked with her, I could feel that she listened as though God and the loving universe was speaking directly to her. I knew she felt safe with me, as though I understood who she was. Early on, it became apparent to my three siblings and me, as well as to the rest of my family, that my mom was mentally ill.

The stress of raising four children without a husband rapidly progressed my mother's schizophrenia. During that time, my extended family, namely my grandparents and aunts, played a large role in helping my siblings and me live normal lives. We attended grade school in Kansas City, Missouri, and were able to participate in song and dance lessons.

My siblings and I became known around our community as the "Holland Four". We performed locally and even had the opportunity to travel to Joplin, Missouri, to help the town celebrate their one-hundredth year anniversary. Our shows were inspiring. Our audiences loved our music and our energy as a family. We would sing and dance and my youngest brother, Rick, would play the drums and the guitar. We also had a pianist accompany our songs. My eldest brother, Mickey, was a singing sensation. His talent was world class and always stole the show. A career in music or show business appeared inevitable for him!

When we performed, it brought magic to our lives and love and fun to our family. Music was our playground! Mental illness had no place during our performances. Our spirits were free. This was a glimpse of what was possible when talent and desire were given a chance. We performed for about five years until my grandfather was suddenly and tragically killed. He was our performance manager; without him, our shows abruptly ended.

Crime increased in our neighborhood during the late 1960s. One night, several years before my siblings and I began to perform musically, my mom was physically assaulted outside of our apartment building. We moved to a more upscale neighborhood, and it seemed as though we had moved from Harlem to Hollywood. We moved from a two-bedroom apartment to a three-bedroom house with a large yard and neighbors who would eventually become some of my closest friends.

After we moved, my mother's illness worsened. She also suffered from asthma. Unfortunately, her asthma was as severe as her schizophrenia. Many times, I lived with the fear that my mom would suffocate. I think this scared me more than any act of physical violence that I witnessed. As a toddler, physical and emotional violence became a common occurrence in our home and in our lives.

My mother would have violent episodes. She would put her fist through glass windows, drive our family car through my grandparents' garage door, slam doors repeatedly, and scream at the top of her lungs over the phone to my grandmother. She would hit my sister, and occasionally my brothers, but she never hit me. I often found myself in the middle of the physical violence, trying to protect my siblings as well as my mother. It was a lot to handle for a child.

Often, I found myself wanting to be hit so I could feel like one of my siblings, so they wouldn't think that I was siding with my mom. I wasn't. It's just that my mom could feel the love in me. Somehow, that protected me from her violence and allowed me to communicate with her—something that was not available to others in my family. Often, I would be asked to talk with my mother when she was distressed in an effort to calm her down and bring normalcy to our home. This continued as I grew into adulthood.

My mother's illness continued to worsen. There were times when I would find her standing in front of a window, staring for days, weeks, and months on end. She had totally disconnected from life, her family, and her children. My grandparents became our parents during that time.

One night, when I was about seven or eight, my mom was taken by ambulance to a psychiatric hospital. Those were some of her worst days. In an effort to help her daughter and four grandchildren, my grandmother would frequently have my mom admitted to a local hospital for psychiatric care. During those times, my grandmother would provide nursing care for my siblings and me. It was a time of great stress. Later, I learned that this was when my personality fragmented as a means of self-protection. This is also known as Dissociative Identity Disorder (DID)—more about that later.

When I was thirteen, my mom decided to move our family home again. It was a time when my siblings and I had no sense of normalcy. My mom's schizophrenia prevented her from performing any motherly duties—cooking, cleaning, or keeping a home. My sister and I moved with my mom, and my brothers decided to live with my grandmother. Eventually, my eldest brother enlisted in the military. A close family friend provided a loving home for my other brother.

This was the beginning of the separation of the family I knew. The following year, my sister moved in with my grandmother, and when my mom was unable to maintain our new home, she had me move in with my grandmother too. Several weeks later, I came home from school to discover that my mom had vanished. This was a turning point in my life.

Following my mom's disappearance, I struggled to stay alive because living with my grandmother was a struggle. It was hard going from a life with no boundaries, no discipline, and no structure to a life filled with heavy structure and discipline and being with a grandmother who was frantic about the whereabouts of her daughter. She tried to help guide the life of her family, but she was under a lot of pressure from running her own business.

One day in the ninth grade, I left school and found myself lying on the side of a hill next to our YMCA. The sun was shining so brightly, and I could feel its warmth resting on my body and in my heart. The sadness that I felt was beyond what most people could comprehend. For hours, I felt the love of the sun and peace on the quiet hill.

I hated school, not because of anything that was happening at school, but because there was so much internal conflict. Trying to focus on learning in the traditional sense was not possible. There were times when I would start fires in my backyard, throw rocks at passing cars, steal food from the local grocery store, and break into the neighbors' homes when they weren't there. I was out of control, yet I very much wanted to be popular, to fit in, and to be someone's friend.

I found some peace when I read *Jordi, Lisa, and David*. Reading the book, I found myself receiving the love these three characters received from their teacher. Jordi, Lisa, and David were diagnosed with emotional disturbances, and their teacher helped them receive the love they had never felt.

One morning, after living with my grandmother for a while, I left her house with a large plastic garbage bag full of clothes and headed for the bus station. I had decided to run away even though I was scared. I did not know where I was headed and had very little money in my pocket.

This was the culmination of years of taking drugs, skipping school, and almost begging to die. I started to smoke pot in the summer of fifth grade. Smoking pot early in life allowed me to feel what other kids felt normally. Years later, when I took drugs, I felt free to talk with others without the worries or sadness that sat on my chest.

My other siblings did not experience the struggles that I encountered, although life for them was not easy either. On the night that I ran away from my grandmother's house, I ended up in a jail cell. I wanted to stay in jail in the worst way because I knew that I couldn't go back to living with my family.

Eventually, this journey took me to the greatest loving environment that I had ever known at that time—a hospital that helped adolescents struggling in life. During the first three weeks, I could feel love in my heart. I made friends with one of my teachers at the hospital, and she soon became my hero. I could feel a love I had only felt once before from my seventh-grade teacher. During those times, I didn't feel the heaviness of my family. I could feel a sense of what I wanted. I felt free to be the person who I came here to be. I was unconditionally cared for.

Then I was suddenly discharged from the hospital due to insurance reasons. Before I knew it, I was back in my grandmother's care and back at school. I went straight from being discharged from the hospital to the front doors of my high school. When my grandmother dropped me off at school, I never went in. I sat under a tree right outside the door that led to my classroom and cried for hours. I was completely lost. I knew that I could not be a student at that point in my life.

My mom had vanished, I couldn't live with my grandmother, and I didn't know where to turn. That night, I told my grandmother that I was going to run away again. She knew that living with her was not possible, and I was admitted to Temporary Lodging for Children. I spent two weeks at the facility before I found what turned out to be my second family in a state group home called Pilot House. During my three and a half years as a resident of Pilot House, I was able to complete my high school education, earn best summer worker out of three hundred applicants, and receive straight A's during my senior year. I was on a roll.

When I first arrived at Pilot House, I finally felt safe. I didn't have to carry the responsibility of helping my mom negotiate her life, and I didn't have to serve as a liaison for my family to help bridge the communication gap between normalcy and mental illness. The group home allowed eight girls to reside there at one time, and there was a staff of six counselors and a director.

Pilot House was a sanctuary for adolescents. It was a port in a very large storm. Emotionally, my life was in turmoil. I had no direction other than downward. Again, I had just come from Temporary Lodging for Children, the state-run facility that housed boys and girls. At Pilot House, I found tremendous comfort in those who surrounded me, especially my counselor. Bob was about ten years older than I was. He had long, straight shoulder-length hair. He was easygoing, loving, and one of my best friends at the group home. Bob and I would spend one hour a week together, privately talking about my life, my struggles, and my accomplishments while I lived there. We often talked about my mom and why she may have vanished during this time in my life.

One day, Bob agreed to take me to visit the house where I grew up, where I had spent most of my time living with my mom and my three siblings. It was about a forty-five-minute drive from the group home, and it wasn't far from my grandmother's house either. When we arrived, Bob went to the front door of the house and knocked.

A lady answered, and Bob asked her for permission to let me walk around the outside of the house. I did so alone. It was difficult. I felt emptiness and a flooding of memories at the same time. So much had happened there. I remembered the animals I had loved while I lived there, my cats Fuzzy and Katy and her little kittens. When I got back into the car, I was unable to talk. I was crying silently, privately, inside. My emotions were hard to share. Where was my mom? Would I ever see her again? We drove back to Pilot House, quietly. It was a very difficult day.

Bob's loving attention seemed to help me the most. I could tell him things that I knew would always be kept private. He was cool. All of the residents and staff loved him too. He had a dog that would live with us when Bob was on duty. Bear was a gentle giant—a beautiful, golden retriever. He was Bob's best friend, and they were always together. I remember one time when one of the residents wanted to go for a walk, a privilege that had to be earned. She asked Bob if she could take Bear with her. When they returned, they were both high on pot. Bob was furious and serious repercussions ensued.

Most of the girls living in Pilot House came from loving, well-intending families, but broken homes. Many of us had probation officers and histories of delinquent behavior. We all struggled in our own ways. Some of the girls would act out their problems, and others were quiet and shy. In the beginning, I fell somewhere in the middle, although with time, I became a house leader. Pilot House gave us a chance to return to society one day.

The staff members were our leaders; since they were somewhat close to our ages, we could relate to them. They always tried their best to meet our needs. They cared so much and seemed to understand our struggles. Many times, the staff would share some of their life struggles with us during our monthly house meetings. These times really brought us together.

When a staff member would retire from the job, it was really hard to see them go. We had become family since the staff lived with us much of the time. When a new member joined the team, it always worked. During my second year living at Pilot House, a new director was hired. Jim and I became good friends over time. He always told me how much he appreciated my kindness when he was new to our facility.

The staff also taught us how to keep ourselves clean, how to pick up after ourselves, and how to cook. Each one of us was responsible for cooking a meal for the group once a week, which was always a challenge for me. They also helped us with our studies. Several of us worked part-time jobs outside of the group home. Working allowed us to earn money and to return to society in a positive way. Often, we all would go to movies together, eat some of our meals out, or have picnics when the weather permitted. And, at summer's end each year, all of the girls and staff members would go on a two-week vacation together! In many regards, we lived just like many families do. Again, it was the loving attention of the staff that mattered most.

We were allowed to attend public school while living at Pilot House. During the late 1970s, drugs were very much a part of the high school scene. While not much different today, it seems like we had less dangerous drugs available to us. I befriended some people who smoked pot, took pills, and drank alcohol. While our friendships were genuine, eventually the drugs became such a problem that the director decided to have me temporarily admitted to the larger institution to which Pilot House was affiliated. I was placed in solitary confinement for one week in a room with one window and a bed—where I was to spend all my time thinking about what I wanted in life.

Incredibly, several years later, I would receive training as an employee at that exact place. The institution relocated and the existing building was sold to a large hospital facility in which I would eventually work. As an adult, I was able to go back and experience that room from a place of progress—where I had been and where I was now headed.

How inspiring to go from being locked in a room—feeling defeated, not knowing how my life would unfold, and not knowing where my mom had vanished to—to walking into that same room knowing that I had come so far as a productive citizen, was able to hold down a job, and could do the job with recognition for outstanding performance. That day lives in my heart and is evidence that life can change even when you are standing within the same walls.

When I look back on Pilot House today, I am forever grateful for the loving family I was given during a time that was chaotic and destructive. The girls I lived with and the staff members who cared for us will always hold a special place in my heart. We shared so much. I believe that the intervention of the group home in my life was a heroic effort implemented by the loving universe to save my life. I was living dangerously and did not care. I had lost hope. With the love of the staff, I began to find my way. I am appreciative for the kind, loving, and dedicated people who work for group homes. I believe that the difference that these shelters make in the lives of those in need is a testament to the agencies and communities who offer these services.

Right before my graduation from high school, my mom suddenly returned after being away for four years. I hadn't seen or heard from her or known her whereabouts that entire time, and I had been so afraid for her.

She had been living in an apartment building in Minnesota and had recently been involved in a fire. She had been an inpatient in a burn unit in Minneapolis. My grandmother flew to Minnesota and brought her back to Kansas City. My mom attended my graduation from high school and was able to visit the group home where I had lived for almost four years. I was glad to see her, but my heart was heavy at the same time. The life that I had come to love at Pilot House—a life of safety, stability, unconditional love, and eventual success in school—was not part of the life I had known with her. My heart was torn for my own life as I moved forward.

Chapter 2

The Universe, My Friend; the Heart of Kindness

Bathing in the Tranquility of the Universe, I Know All Is Well, Always.

As a child, I was always drawn to the outdoors. There, my spirit was free to run and play, and the troubles of my home life were forgotten. I would converse with the universe by giving my love and attention to its beautiful creatures, such as butterflies and ladybugs.

As an adolescent, during times of great stress, I would skip school to find peace sleeping on the side of a hill. To this day, I appreciate the sunshine that warmed my body and comforted me. It was as though the universe provided a warm blanket of love and protection. It was there that I could feel the serenity of a life that I knew was possible. It was there that I never wanted to leave.

As an adult, when I sit in nature for a period of time with a quiet mind, I know the tranquility of the universe and the heart of kindness. The knowing that I always longed for as a child, that all was well, is now within me. In my mind, I can return to the hill that once brought me great comfort and know that I will never have to leave the tranquility that I once found there.

When I moved out of Pilot House, I moved into a dorm room at Oliver Hall on the campus of Kansas University (KU). At eighteen, my life as a ward of the court and living in a group home was behind me. The success I earned while living at Pilot House allowed me to return to the mainstream of life. This was a new beginning. I had left the safety, stability, and boundaries of the group home and was a regular teenager beginning my college career.

At Pilot House, I learned how to be part of a family atmosphere, having dinner and regularly discussing the events of the day, and how to live with others in a way that allowed me to feel good about myself as well as feeling relatively good about those around me. I learned how much I loved being part of a home that didn't have violence and destruction; I enjoyed the love, discipline, and freedom to be who I came here to be. I also realized how much I wanted to be one of the gang, living normally like someone my age. When my housemates and I attended public school, I discovered how much I didn't want to feel different and sensitive just because I lived in a group home.

Since childhood, singing had always been a passion of mine, and the only class I enjoyed during my school years was choir. I remember feeling ashamed having to ask my choir teacher to sign my weekly performance note that the group home required. Actually, all my teachers had to sign one as well.

Because it was obvious that my mom was ill, everyone would stare at her when we would go out in public, which made me feel ashamed. Needing my choir teacher to sign my performance sheet brought back the same shame I felt while out in public with my mom.

I learned that academic success and being a productive citizen are possible when love is present in a healthy way—and stability in the home is consistent and loving. What I didn't realize is that if this love and respect for boundaries is not internalized, then success is short-lived.

During my first semester of college, I quickly found the drug scene again, which meant I struggled to attend class, make passing grades, complete coursework on time, and study for exams. This made being a successful student impossible.

The transition from the group home, where every facet of my life was structured and monitored, to living a life of a college student, where temptation ran rampant, eventually proved to be too much of a challenge. By the end of my first semester, I was placed on academic probation, and over the course of the next three years, I lost all of the federal grant money I had initially received. The drug problem that had begun early in my life was a major hindrance for my success as a college student.

While these first years at KU were some of the hardest, one of the greatest thrills of my life occurred during my first semester there, a time I have never forgotten. I made many friends early on while living in the dormitory. The years I spent in the group home gave me an advantage to this style of living. It was home for me. We were all one big happy family, it seemed, all seven hundred of us. We ate our meals together in the dining hall, studied together when we weren't partying, and attended some of the same classes. It's amazing to see how one's living environment while away from home can truly create a family atmosphere.

There was one guy in my dorm that everyone admired. He was the nicest guy, always smiling, upbeat, and very kind. Dave lived on the top floor and shared a room with a guy I had gone to school with while living in the group home. I had sung with Bob in the high school choir. Now at college, our friendship grew. It was comforting to have a friend from high school standing by my side as we ventured into this next chapter of our lives.

Dave came to KU specifically to focus on architecture. He was an upperclassman at the time, although I never felt much difference in our ages. I was introduced to him at the local donut shop where he worked on weekend nights. He was the guy who actually made the donuts. The donut shop was famous for its hot glazed donuts, which were available at just the right time to satisfy our craving for late-night munchies. I was so happy to finally meet him since our paths had crossed most days while on campus or at the dorm. I never really gave too much thought to dating him, although it was always a highlight of my day to see him. Frequently, I would see him and another girl walking together on campus or in our dorm. They seemed to always be together. They attended many of the same classes, and I would see them at parties as well, which gave me the impression that they were together as a couple.

One particular evening, while I was alone in my dorm room, there was a knock on my door. It was Dave. Needless to say, I was surprised when he asked me if I wanted to go see a movie with him. I nearly fell to the floor. Of all of the persons that I had met during my short amount of time at KU, he was by far my favorite. It was mid-fall, and most of the students were deep into their studies at that point of the semester. Since Dave's weekends were always tied up at the donut shop, I understood why he had knocked on my door on a Thursday evening. I don't remember what movie we saw that night, but I can recall the story that subsequently unfolded between us.

Our first date was simple and fun, just the two of us. We were both shy and quiet, yet there was a genuine feeling of joy and excitement between us. We had so much in common in our personalities and in our spirits that I felt as though I was floating when I was in Dave's company. I had fallen in love overnight. My first impression when I met him at the donut shop didn't come close to describing the kind man that lived within him. He truly was the nicest person.

After our first date, we began to spend more time together, between classes, around Dave's work schedule and our studies. Looking back, one of my favorite things that we would do together was visit a nearby lake. Autumn was in full display, and the love I felt in my heart made for special times while we were together in nature. It wasn't too long before we kissed, and the hours flew by like minutes that first night. What had been late evening instantly, it seemed, turned to early morning—all while "just kissing." Time was irrelevant. The feelings between us grew deeply, very quickly. Sex seemed insignificant and unnecessary. We were so united when we kissed. This never changed.

By far, those were some of the best days of my life, internally. My body chemistry changed. I was weightless. I had many sleepless nights, and any focus I had for my studies almost vanished. Everyone who knew me at the time was aware of my relationship with Dave, especially my sister. For hours, my sister and I would talk. Of anyone in my life, it was my sister who knew how deeply I had fallen in love. My sister and I had a genetic communication. We didn't have secrets. I found great stability with her as I had been completely swept off of my feet. She too admired Dave. In fact, when she visited me at my dormitory after I had moved in, she noticed him first.

We dated for two short months before suddenly, out of nowhere it seemed, Dave began spending time again with the girl who I had seen him with previously. It was clear to me that something had changed. When I didn't hear from him and I would call, he was always so nice and agreeable to get together. Yet, he never came around. Abruptly, our relationship and our friendship ended. It was painful beyond words. Somehow, I understood that I had to let the relationship go. Thereafter, I would see Dave and his girlfriend together often, now holding hands. In my heart, I now understood what she saw in him … kindness, generosity, fun, and love. He was definitely someone to admire in many ways, just as my sister had known so quickly.

Perhaps the most challenging aspect of my relationship with Dave was the short time in which our lives came together so intensively and the suddenness in which it ended. For the first time in my life, I had experienced a loving relationship with a man who I truly admired. Today, I know the standard of love that I wish to bring into my life with the man that I will eventually marry. While my relationship with Dave was short, the quality of our time together has stayed with me, alive in my heart, for all these years.

To fall in love is one of the best feelings in life. It is God's euphoric drug for all mankind. It is to learn what is possible to feel in life when two hearts come together in deep love and passion. Falling in love so deeply is a unity that only the universe can provide; it is a match of hearts that is undeniable and indescribable.

I decided not to return to the dorm for my third year. Instead, I moved into an apartment with two guys who were my age. We had become friends during my first two years at KU. Unfortunately, that year, my drug use escalated. I found myself smoking pot morning, noon, and night, and I was unable to focus on my studies.

I bought sedatives on the street to help me to deal with anxiety, and I took speed to help me deal with the burnout from smoking so much pot.

I also used cocaine and psychedelics when I had the money because those drugs were the best when it came to getting high. Drugs allowed me to become less anxious. They allowed my personality to be free. I felt free to laugh. I was able to fit in socially in a way that I had never known before.

During that time, my sister and I continued to be close. She worked at a satellite library on campus. One of my classes was in that building, and I always looked forward to visiting her, talking with her, and connecting with someone who I believed understood me. I am not sure if I have ever told her how much she helped me psychologically and financially and how grateful I am.

Eventually, I dropped out of college. My youngest brother, who was aware of my struggles with drugs, came to get me and helped me get into a drug treatment center in Independence, Missouri. This was the beginning of many years of continued struggle as I tried to free myself of my drug use so that I might live a life that I could be proud of.

My initial stay at the Independence Sanitarium was somewhat successful. When I was first admitted, I felt as though I had done this before. I remembered what it was like when I moved into Pilot House and when I had been admitted to the psychiatric unit as a young teenager. While in drug rehabilitation, I was able to experience my days without drugs while learning to manage anxiety, sadness, and anger. Again, I felt love from the staff, and I did not have to deal with the stresses of everyday life. I felt that I could become somebody if I could just stay off drugs and find a direction for my life.

While there, I was introduced to Alcoholics Anonymous or AA. For the first time since childhood, I began to feel the knowing or the presence of a higher being. During my younger teenage years, when I would sit on the hill at the YMCA or under the tree at school crying, I never felt the presence of the universe or the presence of an eternal friend, although I did find great comfort there. With Alcoholics Anonymous, I started to feel something that I had never experienced before—hope for my future and feeling a friend who might be with me for eternity. My friend is the universe, the force behind the thought that all is well, my friend who guides me from within.

I began to make friends with others at the sanitarium without the influence of drugs and alcohol as the foundation of our relationships. Once we were discharged from acute care, a group of us began to attend AA meetings together. This group proved to be a strong foundation for me until slowly, eventually, most of us began to use again.

We were mostly professionals, an RN, a fire chief, a couple of construction workers, and myself—a college student. We had all lost our way. Yet, for each other, we could dream of living a quality of life without substance abuse. One by one, it seemed that we all were readmitted into drug rehab. Staying sober and clean proved to be too hard for many of us to maintain during this particular time in our lives.

I also befriended one of the male patients while in rehab. He was very handsome and popular with the staff and the other patients. I was taken by his looks, charisma, and gentle manner. It wasn't long before we were spending time together, usually attending AA meetings. This eventually turned out to be another traumatic event in my life as my relationship with this man tragically ended when he killed himself violently during a night of heavy drinking.

For approximately two years, I continued attending AA meetings and tried to learn how to live a life without using drugs and alcohol.

Chapter 3

The Genius in Schizophrenia

The Tenderness of a Butterfly
Lives within My Heart

Mother, when you would scream and cry and I would hold you, I always prayed for the loving heart within you. When you became angry, violent, and destructive to our home, I prayed for the peace within you. When you became silent and withdrawn and your children could not reach you, I prayed for the capable mother within you. Mother, I have always prayed for you.

And when the violence of your illness was all that I could see and your anger was all that I could hear, I always remembered the tender butterfly that lived within my heart. Mother, today I pray for you. I pray that the illness of your mind will someday give way to the genius of your mind and that the illness of your mind will someday give way to the eloquence of your mind.

Mother, I pray that the tenderness of a butterfly that lives within my heart will never give way to the violence and anger of schizophrenia.

For more than thirty years, my grandmother owned and operated a family business out of her home in Kansas City. She was actually one of the first women to do so in her community. She was a pioneer. In my early twenties, following my treatment at the sanitarium, I began working for her. I needed to make money to supplement the limited income I was making working nights as a dispatcher for an ambulance company. It had been quite some time since my grandmother and I had spent any time together in her home.

The last memory I had of my grandmother's house was when I came home from school to discover that my mother had vanished. This time, coming back was my choice. I was there to help her rather than needing her to take care of me. I began working part-time, helping her with payroll, answering phone calls, and occasionally organizing the work schedules for her staff. I also helped with the housekeeping. I knew she appreciated my attention to detail when it came to cleaning. I worked for my grandmother for about five years as I tried to straighten my ship that had taken a turn for the worse when I left the group home.

When my mother suddenly returned after four years, she lived with my grandmother. Her burns from the building fire in Minnesota required additional medical attention. Eventually, with my grandmother's help, my mom moved into a modest studio apartment. She had recovered from the trauma of the fire, and for the first time in many years, she began working part-time as a receptionist for a dermatologist who was a friend of the family. I was so happy for my mom because I always knew how much she wanted to work.

However, the severity of her mental illness prevented her from holding down a job for very long. She had trouble focusing, which didn't allow her to complete tasks in an orderly way. In addition, she had trouble appropriately socializing with others. I respected my mom during that time. I saw her desire to become a productive citizen. Getting to work was not easy for her. She had to depend on public transportation, and I worried about her taking the city bus since this mode of transportation was notorious for crime. I asked the universe to protect her.

It was hard reestablishing my relationship with my mom after she returned. In the beginning, I was just happy that she was home and that

I knew her whereabouts. I didn't have to wonder if she was dead or alive every night before falling asleep, but my heart was heavy with sadness for her illness and for the effect that her schizophrenia had on our family. After her return, I would ask her why she left for those years without calling or writing. She never could give me a reason, but I knew that her heart was heavy with sadness about leaving.

My mom worked for the dermatologist for a couple of years before she was asked not to return one Friday, right before the Christmas holiday. I was devastated for her; I knew how much the job had meant to her. It was why she got up each day, and I believe her job was one of the highlights of her life. For a person with mental illness, holding down a job is a real accomplishment, even if it is only for a short period.

My grandmother told me that when my mom was in high school, her IQ test rated her genius. As I reflect on my mother's intelligence and the eloquence of her mind, I am better able to know the true person, the woman who lives within the illness of schizophrenia.

Today, I understand and greatly respect the struggle that is my mother's life—living with a genius mind while trying to manage life with a severe mental illness. As I am able to hold close the multitude of talents that is my mother—her physical beauty, her artistic talent, her great communication skills, her passion for life, and her utter determination to live a life of normalcy—I am able to share with myself and with the world the true genius of my mother.

Today, I understand schizophrenia uniquely. My life has allowed it. Organically, schizophrenia is a different wiring. Scientists consider it to be an anomaly in nature, a genetic abnormality. Medically, schizophrenia is classified as an illness, a disease of the mind. According to *The Diagnostic and Statistical Manual of Mental Disorders* (DSM) IV, there are two components to schizophrenia, characteristic symptoms and social and occupational dysfunction. Characteristic symptoms may be hallucinations, delusions, or catatonic behavior. Social and occupational dysfunctions refer to a person's inability to work, relate to others, or remain clean. This is the medical and most popular reference to schizophrenia.

Spiritually, schizophrenia is of a different realm. Those who live with this affliction merely show us that there is another world within our world that is available to us. Just as dogs can hear things that people cannot and birds can see for miles where people cannot, schizophrenia is the same. It is an ability to hear and to see our world in a way most cannot. As Abraham and Jerry and Esther Hicks would say, they merely tune to a different frequency.

To live with schizophrenia is to see life through a different lens and to hear the world through special ears. It is a unique expression of the intelligence in nature. It is a unique expression of man's creativity. There are no mistakes. People who have this "affliction" are here for a reason. They are an expression of the universe. The universe has created them. There is genius in schizophrenia, a creative mind that most cannot comprehend. It is a world all unto its own. It is usually isolated because it is feared and greatly misunderstood.

There is a destructive side to schizophrenia. We often hear about it in the news. Some of us are victims of the violence because we live with it in our families. Others may be innocent bystanders. Yet, the violence, I believe, is a manifestation of the frustrations that they feel from not being able to negotiate both worlds. Those with schizophrenia are caught between those worlds. They can see how we live; at times, they can hear our world too. But often, they live in their own worlds. It is why they do not want to take medication. Their world is normal to them. It just feels right, because it is.

But they are here with us and in essence have become a different breed. How can they fit in and negotiate their worlds inside of our world? Our society tells them what is right for them, for their lives, and for their actions. Their creative minds are dulled with medication. Now they can hear us, and it stops the violence. They are told to now live their lives. Now, they are normal.

Often, those with schizophrenia suffer great physical hardship and illness. They live with many chronic conditions, and many are physically disabled. They live with much resistance to their worlds, and their bodies are a reflection of this distress. Truly, they are heroes, especially those who live well beyond their life's expectancy. Consider the determination that they must embody to stay with us here on earth. How many "normal" people embody this strength?

I often wonder what it would be like if those with schizophrenia could live in a world where only schizophrenia existed and where they could live without the pressures to conform to normalcy. Would the world form around them to ensure their success? Would their creative, genius minds then find their true potential? Would they live more freely from illness? Perhaps their genius minds would far surpass us. Would we be given drugs to live in their worlds?

Did I come equipped organically to hear my mother? Did my life's circumstances force my brain to rewire for my own survival? Perhaps, co-creatively with the universe, I was cared for and guided to discover my own genius within. Ultimately, this allowed the genius of my mother to be fully understood by the genius within me.

At times, I find myself daydreaming. I think of my mother's life without schizophrenia. I can see her physical beauty, as she was when she was younger. I see her with more energy and playful. I can see her going off to work and having a career that reflects her intelligence. I can see her living with a man who radiates her royalty.

I think of what my life would have been like had I not had a mother who embodied schizophrenia, but then I remember the perfection of the universe and trust that all is well and in perfect order. I have greater clarity today about my mother's unique stance in life. I can view her world through the eyes of science and medicine and try to understand what went wrong—or I can choose to see her as my great teacher and see what went unbelievably right.

Soon after my mom was let go from her job, she began volunteering for a local hospital. I knew that volunteering was not my mom's first choice, but it did give her a purpose to get up every morning. It also afforded her the opportunity to socialize with other people her age.

Occasionally, after my grandmother and I had completed our work, we would stop by where my mom was volunteering so we could all go out for dinner. My grandmother loved to eat, and she was always so generous and would pay for our dinner. It was a time of peace for all three of us as well as a sense of love. We would take our time eating, talking about our life events, and feeling as though, at least at this moment, that our family was as normal as the next. I loved to see my grandmother and my mom getting along because I knew that this was not always the case.

My job as a dispatcher led to another traumatic event in my life. The company had changed locations during my employment, and I hadn't done my homework in finding the new place during daylight hours. I found myself wandering the streets late at night. Mistakenly, I pulled into a parking lot that looked like it could be our new building.

To my surprise, a tall, older gentleman opened his car door, walked over to my car, and pointed a handgun at my head.

I held my hands up and said, "Please don't shoot." I was terrified.

He said, "Lady, you almost got shot."

I told him that I was lost and how I was looking for my place of employment.

He let me go, but I never made it to work that night. I never returned to the ambulance company. I was completely traumatized.

My mom moved from her studio into a two-bedroom apartment in a much nicer, safer neighborhood. I had lost my job as a dispatcher, and working for my grandmother was not enough money to pay my rent. So my grandmother, who was paying my mom's rent, suggested that I move in with my mom until I was back on my feet financially. I was, however, afraid to live with her because of the violence, sadness, and destruction I had experienced for years while growing up with her. But I had no choice.

Soon after moving in, I began working at the nearby Shoney's Restaurant. Pretty soon, I was making good money waiting tables and began saving most of it. Before I knew it, I had several thousand dollars. I began taking some responsibility for my life and started paying my grandmother for half of my mom's rent.

Working has always been one of my strongest attributes. My professionalism and attention to detail in whatever job I undertake are talents that were given to me by the universe. My very first job was working at a Putsch's Restaurant in Kansas City. I made good tips for someone my age, and I could feel the ease in which I was able to work. My work success continued as I moved into adulthood.

I worked at Shoney's for approximately three years and was regarded as an employee with a strong work ethic. The customers would frequently share their positive impressions of the quality of my work with my boss. I began to feel a sense of accomplishment that I could hold down a job and do it quite easily. The struggles that I experienced while attending college left me feeling hopeless about my future. The drug treatment center turned out to be a successful transition point in my life; it allowed me to leave the trauma, hardship, and turmoil. At least for the time being, I was beginning to realize that I could do something positive with my life, such as earning my own money and holding down a full-time job. One thing that did not change while I was working at Shoney's was my continued drug use.

One of the worst things about drug use is the people associated with this lifestyle. While working at Shoney's, I befriended a customer who knew one of the other waitresses. I was leery of this guy and knew that I must always have someone with me when I was in his company.

One day, I was to meet him on my street corner to make a drug exchange. While I was standing next to him, I could tell that he was trying to inch his way closer to me. Finally I noticed something sticking out of his left rear pocket with a red handkerchief draped over it. I quickly became frightened and distanced myself from him as we talked. It didn't take long before I ended our conversation and ran back into my mom's apartment. I knew that I had just avoided a very dangerous situation. Today, I believe that he had a knife in his pocket with which he meant to harm me. I'm so appreciative of the universe for protecting me during my time of ignorance.

Chapter 4

A Stalk of Bamboo

The Human Spirit—Say No More

Siblings stand tall in life; you have traveled far. Live with the knowing that the strength of your spirit is the greatest strength that you will ever know.

When we were young, we struggled. We could not comprehend the script of our life's journeys. It was overwhelming, and it broke us apart. For many years, we could not see our future. Today, we have mounted the summit. Our human spirit has prevailed.

Now view the world through the eyes of your wisdom and trust that there is perfection to your life's journey. Recognize the greatness in all of your life's teachings, and you will never again suffer the burden of hardship.

Siblings, welcome each day with appreciation for all that you have lived, and allow the world to know the greatness of your human spirit.

I lived with my mom for approximately two years. The trauma that my siblings and I experienced while growing up with my mom began to rear its ugly head shortly after I moved back in with her. During our childhood, one of the most frightening experiences was the uncertainty of my mom's moods, which affected her behavior.

As her schizophrenia worsened, she became more violent, more often. At night, she would break into our bedroom and beat my sister, which was terrifying. Much of the time, her break-ins would come when we were asleep. Often, I found myself (quickly) standing between my mother and my sister, trying to protect both of them as they hit each other. My sister would hit my mom in self-defense, and my mom would hit my sister for no reason other than she was severely mentally ill.

Now that we were living together again, I noticed that she began to enter my room at night, not to beat me, but to steal the money I was making as a waitress. After work, I would come home and count my tips. I took such pride in counting my money because for some time I had none. I worked really hard as a waitress, and when my mom began to steal my tips, I knew that I must protect my earnings from disappearing. I had to protect myself from her disruptive behavior.

About a year later, my sister found herself needing a place to live, too. She decided to move in with my mom and me. Because the apartment was small, we shared a bedroom. She was involved in a close dating relationship, and her presence at the apartment was part-time. I often found myself wanting her to be home more so we could go out to eat, talk about life, and just be sisters for one another. Nonetheless, I was excited to have her living with us part-time because I enjoyed her company.

Fortunately, we were able to enjoy some happiness together as we were close in age. She was also kind enough to invite me to some of the activities that she enjoyed with her friends.

That winter, we took a weekend bus trip to Vail, Colorado, right before the Christmas holiday. On the way home from Colorado, I was on one of the top beds of our sleeper bus with my back supported by the window. All of a sudden, I felt the window push open and pull me toward the open space. In a split second, I pulled my body forward to avoid falling out of the window. I screamed to my sister, "I almost fell out of the bus." To say the least, my heart was in my throat. To this day, I am not sure why this happened during our trip other than to possibly wake me up to something in my life that strongly needed my attention.

Prior to our trip to Colorado, I experienced the sudden loss of one of my best friends. During my second year in the dorm at KU, I was introduced to a beautiful little kitten. I knew that having pets in a dorm was not allowed, but I felt that I needed to make room for this beautiful little creature. It was toward the end of the school year, and I knew that I would not be coming back to live in the dorm that following year. He was about eight weeks old when I got him, and he quickly became the love of my life. I decided to name him Bamboo because his coat was so beautiful with tan and pale white markings; he truly looked like a stalk of bamboo.

Bamboo and I were inseparable. No matter where I lived, he always had a home. Shortly after my sister moved in with us, I took him to the veterinarian for his routine visit to get his vaccinations.

When we left, the doctor said, "See you in a year."

Within the next twenty-four hours, Bamboo was deathly ill. His stomach had ballooned to the size of a grapefruit, and he was not acting like himself. I returned to the veterinarian within a day and learned that Bamboo had contracted Feline Infectious Peritonitis (FIP).

Within one week, I had to put him to sleep. To this day, I hope that Bamboo forgives me for not being emotionally strong enough to hold him while he made his transition. As he rested in his carrying box, I laid him on top of the counter in the waiting room at the vet and told them to please take care of him. I couldn't handle seeing my best friend leaving me so soon. He was only three and was my closest friend since childhood. Bamboo was laid to rest in a beautiful animal cemetery in Kansas City. I will always remember him for his friendship, his love, and his physical beauty.

After our return from the ski trip to Colorado, I was worried about how the stress of my sister's presence might affect the stability of my mom's mental health. It wasn't long before my mom began to break into our room at night and started hitting my sister. It was no different than what we experienced when we were younger, and the impact was the same. I found myself, once again, standing between my sister and my mother, trying to protect them both from getting hurt. The violence would usually last about five minutes, but the impact has lasted a lifetime.

My sister and I decided to move out of my mom's apartment soon after the nighttime break-ins began. It was hard for me to make the decision to leave because I felt like our presence in my mom's life gave her joy despite her mental illness and the violence that she created.

My sister and I moved into a small house not far from my mom's apartment. The rent was cheap, and the house was big enough that we could cohabitate in a peaceful manner. We realized why the rent was so cheap when we began to find mice in almost every kitchen drawer that we opened. We heard them crawling in the walls at night.

To be honest, we were fond of the home. Its foundation was one hundred feet from a running creek bed, and the property was just outside the boundaries of a city park. The surroundings were peaceful. We lived in the house for about a year until we decided that moving was in our best interests. Actually, we did a good job of pest control by having the house sprayed once a month. By the time we left, the mice were gone!

As I look back on that period of my life, I know that living with my sister, while continuing to work at Shoney's, was a particularly good time. I had found financial stability for the first time since leaving the group home, and I felt as though I was taking control of my life. The one thing that had not changed was my drug use.

On most days, I would smoke pot to help me feel calm, and I enjoyed the company of other people more when I was high. There was something about marijuana that helped me feel less anxious about life and the circumstances that worried me. Today, I understand that the drugs I was taking kept me alive for many years. When I was high, the turmoil, sadness, and self-destructive thoughts that had become such a part of me subsided.

After leaving the house by the creek, I moved into a one-bedroom apartment. I wanted to live by myself. Before leaving our last house, I had "accumulated" my own family who were to be with me for many years. After Bamboo's passing, I purchased a little dog from the local pet store. Charlee was a beautiful, white, miniature Schnoodle. When my sister and I moved out of our mom's apartment, we rescued a cat that had been hanging around our house.

When Kitty first arrived, I would see him at the neighbor's house, not really having anyone to feed or pet him. I soon began to call the cat Kitty, and he would run to me like we had been friends for a long time. Kitty and Charlee gave me a reason to want to live. I always felt unconditional love from them because now I had a healthy outlet for my love.

Soon I was letting Kitty into our house and allowing him to stay the night in order to keep him safe. He was a free spirit just like me, so being outdoors was where he most liked to stay. Kitty began showing up at my doorstep as soon as I got home from work or when I would come outside in the mornings. He was the friendliest stray cat I had ever encountered. There wasn't a mean bone in his body, and I felt like I was the lucky one to have found him rather than he was to find me. Kitty and Charlee matched well. It seemed as though Kitty's life on the street had trained him to adjust to change quickly. Having Charlee around didn't seem to phase Kitty at all.

Charlee, Kitty, and I moved quite a distance from my mom when we left the house by the creek bed. I felt a sense of peace entering my life that I had not experienced before. My new apartment was located in a suburb of Kansas City that was very open and had a country feel to it. I felt as though I had a new beginning. I had never lived alone, but I was gaining confidence in my ability to be self-sufficient. I could tell that something inside of me was changing. I was starting to feel a sense of my adult persona emerging, and I felt excited about my new life. This was new for me. For the very first time, I was independent and able to handle it.

Chapter 5

The Grace of Grandmother

In the Light of Dusk,
the Wisdom of the Day Is Known

Forgive me, Grandmother, for my struggles against you. At the time when you found me, my world was violent and heavy with despair, and this is all that I knew to show you. I was only trying to find my way.

Now, wherever you may be, I can show you the wisdom of my life's journey, just as the light of dusk displays for me the wisdom of each day. When I stand in the light of the universe, I can see more clearly the person you were. I am able to appreciate your life's great struggles and admire the successful woman you were. I have learned much from your life's journey. Your teachings will always be alive in my heart.

Today Grandmother, I love you more than ever.

One day, my sister-in-law informed me that there was a more prestigious waitressing job open at TGI Friday's. She had been working there for several months and said that I would enjoy the camaraderie that was common among the staff. TGI Friday's was an up-and-coming restaurant chain then, and they were known to have good food and good benefits for their employees. I quit my job at Shoney's, and I was eager to make the change.

Once I began working at Friday's, I felt as though I had made a significant change in my life professionally. I was beginning to think that I might be able to return to school. I continued to work for my grandmother part-time; her business continued to perform well, and she needed my help. For as long as I can remember, my grandmother's business was a mainstay in our family. Each one of us, at some point in our lives, assisted my grandmother with her business—my two aunts, my sister, my mom to some degree, and my brothers. It was a family affair.

My grandmother had a wonderful reputation and was respected for how hard she worked. I appreciated her commitment to her business. She taught me that owning and operating a business is a lifetime achievement that can be very empowering, especially as a woman. There are not many people who can say that they were in business for more than thirty years, especially during an era when a woman working in her home was almost unheard of.

While my grandmother's commitment to her business was unique, I now understand that her commitment was really for the success of her family. Had my grandmother not worked as hard as she did, the life that we knew as children would have had a much greater traumatic impact on all of our lives.

My employment at TGI Friday's was successful and lasted for about three years. As I had experienced at other jobs, I found myself regarded as one of the stronger employees and earned the respect of management. While still working at TGI Friday's, I transitioned from waitressing to being a food expeditor, a position that is responsible for dressing the dinner plate before it leaves the kitchen. I enjoyed that aspect of food service; I had tired of the daily grind of meeting the needs of the public, yet I wasn't ready to leave the business.

During my first year at Friday's, I decided to return to KU. Even though I was busy working two jobs, both jobs were relatively easy, and returning to school part-time seemed doable. I wanted to complete what I had started in the fall of 1980. In the back of my mind, I knew that completing my education was an important aspect for my future success. My relationship with my grandmother and my mom was better than it had been at any time in my life. However, my mother's schizophrenia was still very much a part of her life and mine as well.

Because I was working for my grandmother, I continued to see my mom. The relationship between my grandmother and mother was stressful. I could feel that they both loved each other, but because my mother refused all attempts by my grandmother to help her, their relationship was strained. The violence that my mom would direct at her children would also be directed toward my grandmother, my grandfather, and my mom's two sisters. It was a lot to handle.

There is one day that stands out in my mind, and it is not easy to write about. It was an incident that occurred when I was living with my grandmother right before my mom vanished. One afternoon, my mother was very upset and angry toward my grandmother. Usually her anger centered on an event that caused her to feel as though my grandmother was taking her children away from her, which was never the case. I remember seeing my mom's face distorted with anger as she stood in the kitchen, swearing at my grandmother.

Very early, I learned the looks that would come across my mother's face when she was experiencing an exacerbation of her mental illness. This particular afternoon was no exception. As I often did, I found myself standing to the side of my mom, ready to intercept any violence that would erupt during her angry rages. I looked toward my mother and asked her not to speak to my grandmother in that way, and she suddenly spit in my grandmother's face. For a brief moment, my grandmother stood still, speechless. I said nothing. I was frozen in fear. My mother continued swearing at my grandmother, and then she turned to her left and began putting her fist through the dining room windows. Once my mom had injured herself, the violence and anger would begin to subside.

As an adult, I recognize that mental illness knows no boundaries. Even though my mother's IQ is so high, because she was unwilling to take medication without involuntary confinement, there was little that our family could do. Of all the things I experienced as a child, intercepting acts of violence was one of the hardest things I had to do.

With all of the distress of my mother's illness, I was still able to focus on my studies when I returned to KU for the fall semester in 1987. I knew that I wanted to be successful, and I decided to take two courses that would ensure my success. When I began my college career in 1980, earning a degree in psychology and journalism had been my passion. However, I learned how difficult it would be for me to earn those degrees, considering the high-level courses I would have to take and pass.

The education that I had received prior to my college years had become a hindrance for me. My inability to concentrate left me with a huge education gap that I was now beginning to realize. Since my earliest years, attending school and focusing was something that was just not possible for me. Starting in the first grade, I began to skip class. I often found myself wanting to wander the streets rather than sitting in a classroom. My mind could not handle the confinement of school.

Instead, I would take my lunch money, walk down to the drug store, and buy all the candy I could afford. I did this for a short time before I was caught. I remember sitting in the principal's office while still in the first grade, listening to my mom and the principal scold me for my actions, but I knew deep inside that I was not going to follow a typical path.

Since I was five, I knew that I needed to walk my own path. I couldn't hear the universe when I sat in school. However, the call was so strong in me; I had to listen, although I didn't understand this back then. Those who surrounded me tried to guide me toward what they knew to be right for my life. They wanted me to be a typical student and to attend class, but that would take me away from my inner calling. I was in turmoil, and I struggled. I knew back then that something, an intelligence that lived within me, was real.

While still in first grade, it also became apparent that my inability to concentrate extended to my home. When our family would sit down to dinner, I often would jump up from the table, jump over the wall of our first-floor balcony, and run to the top of our neighbor's hill to listen to the ambulance or police sirens. This urge in me was so strong. There was knowledge there. Through the sirens, I was reading the universe. I would just sit and listen, staring at the sky. I loved what I heard. I felt so connected. That was something I did until we moved out of that neighborhood.

To succeed in college, I knew that I had to customize my education to fit the history of my prior experience. I decided to go for a bachelor's degree in general studies (BGS). I learned during my first semester at KU, when I enrolled in my first foreign language class, that if passing a foreign language was necessary for me to earn a college degree, then I was probably not going to finish college.

As it turned out, earning my BGS degree did not require a foreign language. I could focus the bulk of my studies on psychology, which would prove to be very important when I progressed in my professional career.

I was relatively stable while I was working for my grandmother, working at Friday's, and attending college part-time. This was the most successful I had been, both personally and professionally, since my senior year in high school.

Living by myself with my cat and dog, I found that I enjoyed attending college when my course load was light and I didn't feel overwhelmed with the stress of studying. I appreciated the fifty-minute drive from Kansas City to Lawrence, Kansas, where my classes were held. This gave me time to relax and enjoy nature. The speed of my life was pretty fast; any opportunity I had to slow my pace and take a breather was greatly welcomed. No longer was I living on campus and exposing myself to the many temptations associated with that lifestyle. I knew all too well how it affected me. I made friends with a couple of my neighbors in my apartment complex, and I began to feel like Kansas City was home for me. I was beginning to find a new direction, one that was positive and conducive to building my future success.

I continued to see my mother frequently. She would call my grandmother's house when I was working there to talk with my grandmother, usually about her need of money, or to talk with me. Consistent communication between us seemed to be of significance for her overall mental stability. I, too, wanted to talk with my mom, but I also knew that when I distanced myself from her for any length of time, the destructive thoughts and depressed feelings that had been with me since childhood would lessen. I was torn between wanting her happiness and stability and concern for my own wellbeing.

At Friday's, I was able to make friends with some of the wait staff and employees. In particular, I befriended a hostess. Kelley and I were close in age, petite, and enjoyed spending time together.

My relationship with Kelley eventually led me to one of the most beautiful moments of my life when I witnessed the delivery of her baby. Kelley had been involved with a man who was not completely supportive of her. When she became pregnant, I knew that the challenges she experienced in her relationship were not healthy for the baby or her. I offered my support, and we agreed that I would be her labor coach and attend Lamaze classes with her. On November 11, 1988, Kelley delivered, by an emergency C-section, a little girl. When I witnessed the birth, I knew that my friend had given me a gift of a lifetime.

While working at Friday's, my struggles with alcohol began to worsen. It was common for the staff to enjoy a beer or two after a hard day's work. It also seemed that those impromptu parties enhanced the camaraderie of the restaurant. Many of my shifts were in the evenings since I tailored my work schedule around my classes and working for my grandmother.

After work, I would often stay at the bar too long and drink too much to drive home safely. One night in particular, I was driving home drunk when a police officer pulled me over. I cannot remember what the police officer said to me, but I do remember that as soon as I saw the flashing red lights in my rearview mirror, any troubles that I was experiencing due to alcohol intoxication vanished. I was sober in a second, and I was able to tell the officer that I had just gotten off work and was very tired. I must have been convincing because the officer let me go without a ticket. To this day, I am thankful for the impact that event had on the rest of my life. I was fortunate enough to learn, without tragedy, that drinking and driving can be a deadly combination.

It wasn't too long after that incident that I began seeking professional help in an effort to understand why I needed drugs and alcohol to deal with my life. I started seeing a counselor at the Guidance and Counseling Center at KU. I found some of the counselors to be helpful, but I knew that I needed more.

I had always known that my knowledge or connection with the universe and my connection with infinite intelligence were strong, although I became separated from this connection during my teenage years. It was what my mother sensed in me as a child and what had protected me against her acts of physical violence. I needed to meet someone who could connect with my inner intelligence and who could appreciate where I had been—someone who would understand the chaos and violence I had experienced growing up and could help me sort out my internal struggles.

As I successfully attended my classes, worked part-time at Friday's, and worked for my grandmother, one thing became apparent. I was able to focus in school much better than at any other time in my life. In fact, I was amazed by how much I enjoyed learning and how much learning helped me keep my mind off troubling thoughts.

It was as though class time and studying gave me a timeout from life, and I could get lost in my studies and begin to feel good about myself. Once I began to consistently make good grades, I realized my passion for learning and gave more time to my studies. I read the newspaper daily and focused in a way that was not possible during my childhood. While moving forward, I continued attending counseling sessions at the Guidance and Counseling Center. The concerns that had bothered me were my mom's mental illness and the verbal, emotional, and physical violence. The stress associated with her illness seemed to always be with me.

I also carried the sadness of my friends who had recently committed suicide—my roommate from Pilot House, my boyfriend from the sanitarium, and one of the boys I had lived with during my third year at KU. All three friends were significant at some point in my life, and their deaths still live with me. Like me, they all had loving hearts that were heavy with sadness. It brought us together and eventually separated us.

When I learned of their deaths, I told myself that when I reach the other side, the side where sadness and despair do not live, I will fully release their spirits from my heart into the world so that they may somehow feel the relief that they had always been looking for. All three left me with a desire to better my life so that somehow, through me, they could experience the success that had escaped them. I knew that their deaths were wake-up calls for me to choose a different path.

In 1989, my path began to change. When the fall semester concluded at KU in 1988, I decided not to return to the counselor that I was seeing. I could feel that the heavy load in my heart was not being fully addressed. I knew my concerns were not the typical issues that were discussed with just any counselor. I asked the universe to assist me in my search for someone who could understand and who could help me live a different life. On the inside, I felt a horrendous sadness that had been building for years.

On Thursday, January 5, 1989, at eleven o'clock in the morning, I met Denise L. Gulledge, PhD. Two weeks prior to meeting her for the first time, we had spoken briefly on the telephone. I had been given the names of two different psychologists from one of my college instructors. I called both of them and left messages for them to return my call.

Denise returned my call, and as we were closing our conversation, she said, "I'm here if you need me." Once I heard her words and, more importantly, when I felt her words in my heart, I knew that I would be calling her back.

The day I walked into Denise's office, I told her that I was looking for someone to talk to and that she had to be smart enough or I would not be coming back. I was already at the end of the line talking with counselors at school about my problems. My counseling days began when I was eleven years old when my grandmother insisted that I see a psychiatrist to help me deal with my problems and to help me stop taking drugs. As a teenager, I had a counselor for every year of my life, from the psychiatric unit at the hospital when I was fourteen to counselors at my school, at Pilot House, and at the drug rehabilitation units when I was in my late teens to my early twenties. I always felt as though I was smarter than all of them combined, although my life didn't reflect that. I told myself that if Denise was not able to help me, I was not going to search any longer for help. I was going to quit and find my answers elsewhere.

Chapter 6

Primary Gift

Meditation
Is
Love Returned

"Close your eyes and go inside," Denise said. "Sit quietly and ask the wise one for the answer. What do you get?"

For more than twenty years, I always said, "Horrendous sadness, Denise. When I go inside, I feel a rock sitting on my chest. It is black, it is heavy, and it keeps me from breathing. It covers my heart, it won't let you in, and it won't let me out. It is all that I know."

And for more than twenty years, Denise always said, "Take a deep breath, and let the sadness move through you. Allow your arms to hug the sad parts within you, and let them know the love that you hold for them. Now sit quietly, and tell me what you notice."

Today, I notice the love that has become my own. I notice that when I sit quietly and listen, my wise one tells me that all the love I could ever want is always there for me to receive. Through meditation, I know that I am the receiver of all the love from within my own heart.

Within five minutes of sitting down in Denise's office, I began to sense what I had felt on the phone during my initial conversation with her. She was different and the level of expertise, knowledge, and caring she provided would set her apart from what I had previously experienced. As I sat down, she handed me a welcome letter, which stated what she looked to provide was a caring atmosphere as we explored my concerns. Based on her letter, I could feel in my heart that she could truly provide what she communicated. Looking back, I loved her approach at our first meeting. It was a cool way to let me know what I could expect.

From that first day, I felt no worry or concern about how she would receive me as a client. I didn't even know if I was going to hire her as my therapist, given all of the counseling I previously had and given the saturation point in which I found myself with the entire process. Yet, I knew that I still needed help. As I began to share why I had come, I told her I was looking for someone who was smart enough to work with me and that I was tired of being the counselor in my other counseling relationships.

Through my years of dealing with my mom, I had developed a very keen sense of discernment and reading people because my survival depended on it. My mother's illness put me on high alert very early, which required me to focus in a way that was not required of most people. I recognize now that what I have learned in just a few years is, perhaps, what others learn during a lifetime. I knew I had come here to be a teacher.

Over the years, as Denise and I talked about our first day together, she retells the story that she remembers. At some point during our initial visit, I stood up and walked toward the door to leave. As I did, she said, "I am smart enough to work with you." She knew she only had a few seconds to stop me or I might never come back. She also told me she loved that I was full of piss and vinegar and how I was the only one who entered her office and spoke as I did during their first therapy session.

My life changed that day. I remember feeling a sense of shock and relief for the work that was to come with Denise as I went back to work at my grandmother's. I knew in my heart I had found someone to talk with on a level that I had not found before. My grandmother was aware that I was going to meet my new counselor; when I returned, she asked how it had gone. I told her I believed that I had met someone very special. I wasn't able to say much more, but what I felt in my heart was hope for my future, and for an eventual release of my sadness and despair. It was ready to pour out. I also felt hope that the responsibility of my mom's illness that I carried quietly inside could now be shared.

On my second visit, I walked in and sat down. Denise said, "What are you feeling?"

I remember feeling so much sadness that my defense mechanisms kicked in, and I was unable to share what I had needed to share for years. That sadness has guided my therapy with Denise for more than twenty years.

I also knew that working with Denise was not going to be financially easy. The charge was sixty-five dollars an hour back then; as a student with two part-time jobs, I wasn't sure where the money was going to come from. I told myself if I could find a way to make this happen financially, I would become the person I always knew I could be. I also told myself that if I were to invest the money, I could no longer take hard drugs. I knew I didn't want to sabotage my efforts. Within one month of starting my work with Denise, I had discovered that my medical insurance through Friday's would help pay for my counseling.

Within three months of starting therapy, I dropped out of school again. Due to therapy, I could feel the turmoil developing inside of me. I was unable to focus completely at school, and barely at work. Therapy was consuming all my energy.

Denise told me that sometimes you have to go back before you can go forward, and that is exactly how I felt. At the time, one of my brothers was working as a paramedic for a large hospital chain in Kansas City. He was also working part-time and finishing school so that one day he could realize his dream of becoming a doctor. He suggested that I apply for a full-time position the hospital had in the patient transportation department. I had never worked in healthcare, let alone a very large hospital, and I was a little nervous about taking the position. I trusted my brother, and sure enough, his advice turned out to be another turning point in my life, professionally. Healthcare is where my life's work would eventually take me.

I remember how excited I was to wear white scrubs as my new uniform. It felt so official. My main responsibility was to courier medical items, such as lab specimens, blood products, and patient medical pumps, between the different departments of the hospital, although I was officially working in patient transportation. I knew that the universe was supporting me. Had I been responsible for transporting patients every day, given my small size, I wouldn't have lasted very long.

In other ways, the job turned out to be a perfect fit for me. It didn't require intense mental focus for extended periods of time. I knew in my heart that working in patient transportation was a starting point for what I wanted in life. I did my job with appreciation and respect. I was so happy to make the transition from working in food service to serving the public in healthcare. Another benefit of leaving the food industry was leaving behind the temptation for heavy drinking with coworkers following work. I was happy to not be in an environment conducive for drinking.

My grandmother allowed me to adjust my work hours for my new job while continuing to work for her. My duties for my grandmother involved paperwork and accounting. However, another aspect of it was talking with her staff and the families of those she served. I learned from my grandmother that how you treat your employees and your clients determines your overall success. She showed me that your employees are every bit the client, just in a different way.

I continued my therapy weekly and soon discovered that working for my grandmother, and being involved with my mother's care, was becoming increasingly uncomfortable for me. I found it difficult to discuss my family's challenges. My grandmother was very much involved in the day-to-day comings and goings of my mom's life. She took on the responsibility of financing my mother's life as well as providing transportation to and from the grocery store and the like.

She would also attempt to schedule psychiatric appointments for my mom in an effort to help her improve the condition of her schizophrenia.

Occasionally, my mom would comply, but it never lasted long. This was an ongoing struggle between my mom and grandmother.

My family, from my mom's sisters to my grandparents, would try to assist my mom in getting the help she needed. But, as is the case with many mentally ill people, my mom would become angry and violent with everyone who persisted in trying to help her. My grandmother's involvement in my mother's life continually exposed her, our family, and me to the stress of mental illness. My therapy allowed me to recognize the toll that my mother's illness had taken on the totality of my life.

For approximately three years, I worked in patient transportation. During that time, I made great progress in my therapy. I could feel a sense of trust building in my relationship with Denise that I had never known before. I began to understand the significance of personal boundaries, where a person stops and another begins. In families with mental illness or dysfunction, boundaries are commonly not developed or respected. And boundaries between a mother and daughter, whether in a healthy relationship or not, can many times be unclear. This is when a child can begin to feel the heaviness of a mother's illness. The child does not know what her responsibility is and what that of the parent is. For many children, this can be the beginning of many years of suffering and turmoil, just as the case was for me.

While my understanding and development of personal boundaries was a significant undertaking during my initial therapy, my learning of the power of respect for self, for others, and for life was equally important. From day one, I was very aware of and impressed by the way Denise held herself—the way she sat, stood, and walked through life. I remember taking note of the clothes she wore and the way she began and ended our sessions. Everything spoke of professionalism and respect. She conveyed an awareness of her knowledge of where she left off and where I began.

Very early in our relationship, I thought, *I'll have what she is having*. She had congruency between what she taught and how she lived. I began to understand the enormity of the work we would eventually undertake. The gap between where I had come from and where I wanted to go became clear.

Often when Denise and I met, I struggled with feelings of nervousness, anxiety, and sadness. For years, I had taken drugs to help me feel relaxed and to deal with my life's issues. I knew there was no room for drugs during therapy if I was to change my life. I was determined to give myself a chance to live my life differently, although it was not easy. The urge to take drugs and medicate my mind was a force within me. That was something I didn't understand until I eventually relocated outside of the Kansas City area.

It was important for me to share all the sadness, disappointment, anger, and fear with Denise. Yet my inner defenses to feeling and releasing any of this emotional turmoil had become impermeable. It was hard for me to look at Denise for any length of time when we talked, and I found it challenging to stay seated during our sessions. As a child, I'd always had a lot of energy, and staying in one place for any length of time was difficult. One of the things I appreciated about Denise was her willingness to allow me to do anything in her office that would help me feel more comfortable with our work. I began to bring putty to our sessions in a plastic egg. It became one of the most comforting aspects of my therapy over the years. Using the putty allowed me to discuss matters with Denise while I discharged some of my energy and stayed focused on the topic at hand.

As I continued my therapy, I transitioned from patient transportation to the admitting office at St. Luke's Hospital. My recent success as a transportation technician allowed me to develop a sense of confidence in my ability to focus, and I knew I would need this to move forward professionally. I also knew that a step up in my responsibilities within the hospital was right for me.

My brother, once again, was instrumental in having me apply for the admitting clerk position. Again, my trust in him was warranted. As it turned out, working in the admitting office was the perfect job as my interest in returning to school at KU became apparent. I was working the evening shift in the admitting office, and going back to school would fit into my schedule. I decided to cut back on my hours with my grandmother and began to shift my focus to completing my bachelor's degree. My life was showing signs of improving.

I knew in my heart that this time around I had returned to KU to finish the degree I had began in 1980. Completing my bachelor's degree was just the tip of the iceberg of what was possible for me academically. For most of my life, being successful as a student was not possible, but now my focus had changed. I was building a foundation of stability, love, and trust with Denise, and I was more at peace internally. Becoming a successful student would allow me to one day realize all my dreams. It was essential that I complete a higher-level degree, such as a master's degree or even a PhD. I had begun to look into physical therapy programs at the same time I was considering going back to school.

Becoming a physical therapist would allow me to combine my interests in psychology, sports, and medicine. It felt like a perfect fit. I knew that completing my bachelor's degree with the highest grades possible was a top priority. When I returned to KU, my GPA was a cumulative 2.0. I knew that to have a chance of getting into any postgraduate program, I needed to raise it.

Knowing what I needed to do, I became committed to my education. When I sat in the student advisor's office discussing my academic situation, she told me that I must make straight A's in all of my remaining classes as an undergraduate to have a chance at postgraduate studies. I knew I could rise to the occasion because my future depended on it. I wanted to become a physical therapist.

My interest in physical fitness, health, and medicine began while I was working at Friday's. Looking back, I understand one of the most significant outcomes of my employment there was being introduced to long-distance cycling and where it would eventually lead me. I had befriended several of the wait staff involved with the local chapter of the MS Society.

At the time, they were looking to recruit riders who could train and eventually complete a 150-mile bike ride in two days. My friends had been involved with the MS charity event for several years and were successful in raising thousands of dollars. I was inspired to meet the challenge and to help them in their efforts to raise money.

My true love of sports actually began in the mid 1960s when our hometown Kansas City Chiefs, were one of the premier football teams.

I was the only one in my family who watched the Chiefs defeat the Minnesota Vikings to win Super Bowl IV. It was then that I discovered my passion and excitement for sports, the energy of winning, and the grace with which the athletes performed. I knew there was something about sports that rang true in my heart.

For five consecutive years, I rode in the MS150. Training for that two-day event was a yearlong commitment and another turning point in my life. I learned the discipline of focus, and I could feel my confidence grow in other areas of my life. My mind became sharper with all the training.

My love of cycling eventually gave way to weightlifting and long-distance running. I ran my first marathon in the fall of 1993. I remember there was no one happier for me than my grandmother. For years, I had struggled to make something of myself, and she knew how important it was for me to complete the marathon.

Months before the marathon, I knew that if I could find the discipline to train for and complete a twenty-six-mile race, then I could accomplish anything I put my mind to. I was starting to believe.

During the week leading up to the race, the weather had been changing. Winter was beginning to fill the air. The day of the marathon, the starting temperature was seventeen degrees. I had been training for the marathon all summer, and I didn't have much experience running in cold weather. I was determined to finish, and I knew that nothing would stand in my way. I dressed in layers to accommodate the temperature change, but as it turned out, the temperature never climbed above twenty-five degrees. I completed the marathon in four hours, twenty minutes—reaching my first real goal in life.

Perhaps of greater significance during the race was an event that happened around the seventeen-mile marker. My grandmother had been aware of all of the training I had been doing, and she told me that she wanted to support me on the day of the run. Since it was the coldest day of the season, I knew the weather would be a deterrent for many who wanted to take part in this yearly event. I had spoken with my grandmother the night before and knew there was a good chance the cold would keep her away. She was getting older and had a difficult time breathing in cold weather due to her asthma. I knew she was so proud that I had undertaken this challenge and that it would mean a lot for her to see me running in the race.

I was well past the halfway point, and I was beginning to struggle physically. My legs were tight, my feet were sore, and there wasn't one inch of my body that was not cold. I hadn't seen my grandmother along the path, and I had concluded that the weather was too cold for her to tolerate for any length of time. I also knew I had to stay mentally tough to complete the race. I had taken pleasure from the people who did brave the cold and were cheering us on along the way. You never truly appreciate the kindness of strangers until you recognize that their acts of kindness allow you to become your best.

The marathon course took a close turn toward the neighborhood where my grandmother lived, and I was beginning to sense I might have a visitor standing at the top of the hill. The elementary school was just down the road from my grandmother's home. As I ran past Somerset Elementary School, on my left hand side, my grandmother was dressed in all her winter gear, cheering me on. It was only for a brief second that we crossed paths, but this intersection has stayed with me. Before my grandmother passed away in 2005, she said, "Keep your word." She taught me what it feels like to be the recipient of someone who keeps his or her word.

Training for the marathon was significant. I began to understand the power of health and fitness and the role that each played in helping one lead a successful life. Physical training helps a person develop self-confidence and self-esteem as well as learning how to focus diligently and consistently. My interest in weightlifting, running, and cycling eventually led me to take part in cross training, and eventually to participate in local triathlons. Physical fitness had taken center stage in my life, and due to that, all aspects of my life were flourishing. I had developed a love and discipline for physical health.

In another way, physical fitness was divine intervention. When I exercised, my body released tension and my mind relaxed—something I had always turned to drugs for. I was starting to learn a new way. It wasn't until years later that Denise and I fully understood the role drugs and alcohol had played in protecting me from my inner chaos and despair. With physical training, my social circles also changed. I began to associate myself with others who integrated health and well being in their lives. This was paramount for my future success and maintaining my new direction in life.

Chapter 7

Finding Her Here

Vibrational Sensitivity,
My Truest Intellect

Be still. Listen. The universe is speaking. Do you know its language? It lives within you. It is your first language and your guiding light. Gentle being, with heart, you do hear, you do communicate, and you do have intellect. With heart, you are sensitive to all matters of the universe, and you beat as one with the heart of the universe.

Gentle being, since childhood, you have known the truth of your first language as though it was all that you could ever hear, as though it was all that you had ever known. Since childhood, you have known the truth of your vibrational being and the truth of your loving heart.

Gentle being, be still and listen. The universe is speaking. With heart, you will know the truth of your first language and your guiding light. With heart, you'll know your truest intellect.

When I returned to school, I realized my focus for my studies was benefiting from all of my physical training and recent athletic accomplishments. I had developed a keen sense of discipline and could see the evidence with the grades I was earning. I hadn't been a successful student since my last year of high school; now I was successful because I was able to concentrate. In May 1996, I graduated from Kansas University with a bachelor of general studies degree.

It had taken sixteen years to finally graduate from college, and there were many times during those years when I wasn't sure if that day would ever come. Graduating was a significant accomplishment in my life, and I was eager for more. I was beginning to build momentum, and I could feel what was possible for the future. In many ways, those sixteen years were the hardest of my life, and I knew I still had a long road ahead of me. I also knew my budding love for school and my studies was probably my ticket to the life I had always dreamed of.

As I think back to my graduation from KU, I remember what a special day that was—for my entire family. My family was happy for my success, and they were also happy for the success of my brother. Rick was graduating from KU's medical school, a major milestone in his life. He, too, had a life of great challenges, and when he graduated, I knew he had come a long way. I respect him so much for his journey and for his accomplishments. When my brother and I walked down the hill to receive our diplomas, a long-standing tradition at KU, I knew it was significant for our entire family.

Before graduation, my brother and I had discussed the appropriateness of our mother attending the ceremony. In our hearts, we wanted to share our special day with her and to give her one of the joys of being a mother. We wanted her to know that our success was her success. We knew she had continued to decline with her mental illness. We were unsure of her mental stability and didn't want the day to end in trauma.

Against our better judgment, we decided to invite her. We had hoped the celebration would allow our mom to have a day of reprieve from her illness. Unfortunately, as the day unfolded, any laughter and joy gave way to the physical violence and anger that is so prevalent with schizophrenia.

It was evident that our mother's illness was still very much a part of life in our family. As it turned out, during the next couple of years, my brother and I would eventually assist our mother in obtaining the help she so desperately needed and which she had so vehemently fought against for many years.

In the two years following my graduation, I attended classes at a community college and was able to successfully complete the additional coursework necessary to apply to physical therapy schools. That work included several high-level college courses, such as chemistry, physics, and statistics, as well as a course in public speaking. I had never taken courses like that, but I knew the discipline I had developed to complete my bachelor's degree was going to benefit me; I was determined to be accepted into a reputable physical therapy program.

In the fall of 1997, I applied to the physical therapy program at Rockhurst University in Kansas City, Missouri. Perhaps one of the most memorable moments during my application process came during the on-site interview. One of the steps required for all applicants was to participate in a series of interviews with faculty members and other student applicants. Surprisingly, I felt as though the interview process would help identify me as a strong applicant.

Being able to communicate has always been a strong point for me. My communication skills allowed me to shine professionally, and my mom's illness helped me develop a keen sense of the impact of language on the feelings of others. I knew that my word choice allowed me to build trust with her in a way others couldn't. Now, as a student, I knew in my heart that if I could successfully receive an invitation for an interview, I felt confident about my chances for acceptance into a program.

There was a point during one of my first interviews when I began to feel confident that I might have landed one of the available spots. I was seated to the left of two other students, and there were two faculty members seated in front of us. The circumstances for the interview might seem intimidating, but I felt on the same level as the instructors. Maybe it was for no other reason than I was closer in age to the faculty than the other students were. I was thirty-six.

The male faculty member asked me to tell him something important about myself. I began to talk of the discipline of fitness and the benefits of training. I talked about how much confidence I had gained through years of physical training and competing in a marathon and several triathlons.

As I was answering his question, I could see in his face and eyes that I had gained his attention and respect. I sensed he could feel the personal empowerment I had developed through all my years of training. I could see my answer helped shine the light on my determination to succeed.

In the spring of 1998, I received a letter from Rockhurst University stating that I had been accepted into the physical therapy program, class of 2001. There were about three hundred applicants. I was one of forty accepted. I had turned a corner. I had been accepted into a master's-level program, and I was determined to succeed.

I was excited for the opportunity to learn all about the body and spend time in studies that would mean something for my future. I knew financially that entering physical therapy school was going to be a hardship, but just as I learned when I began with Denise, when you are on target with your life, the universe shows up in ways that you can never imagine.

As it turned out, one of my mom's sisters, my aunt, and her husband were aware of my financial situation. Without asking, they generously decided to help finance my physical therapy education. My aunt and uncle said, "Kelly, you are a good investment." They knew of my potential. They believed in me. To this day, they have stood by my side, encouraging me and supporting me to become my best.

My life was unfolding beautifully, but the feelings of sadness and despair that began during my childhood continued to affect me. My work with Denise was intense; after many therapy sessions, I would need several days before I could fully refocus my attention on my studies. But, because my love for the human body, my love for physical fitness, and my desire to become a physical therapist was so strong, maintaining my ability to focus on my studies was paramount.

My determination to stay in therapy during my master's degree program was just as strong. In my heart, I was hopeful that the foundation I was building would some day give way to success beyond my wildest dreams. Yet, I was not fully aware of the upcoming years of therapy and the amount of determination I would need to succeed.

As Denise and I continued our work together, it became clear to us that I had developed Dissociative Identity Disorder (DID). This disorder develops in situations that involve repeated levels of high stress and does not allow full integration of all the parts of the personality. It can take many years of working with a highly trained professional to allow the personality to fully re-integrate as one. As Denise explained, a healthy personality is like a rich bowl of soup, with many different types of ingredients and where all of the parts of the soup come together to create a magnificent whole. And while this integrated soup may contain separate ingredients that are bitter or sour, when combined with the ingredients of sweetness, the soup becomes a rich, magnificent blend of all of its parts.

When DID is present, there is no soup. There are just separate ingredients, operating individually, at different times, and with different outcomes. And while one ingredient may be wonderfully delicious, many of the other ingredients, when operating alone, can be quite the opposite. This means there is a lot of internal chaos.

As I began to understand DID, I realized why, for so many years, I felt as though I was a twelve-year-old operating in a maturing woman's body. And, at times, it was as if I was a ninety-year-old living in the body of a child. I knew I had the wisdom of someone beyond my years, but I felt young, awkward, and different than my peers most of my life. I only felt at ease when I would get high.

My work with Denise showed me how my personality fragmented in childhood and how I had become stuck in my childhood and adolescence due to the traumatic stress I experienced when I was young. At the same time, I began to appreciate how the lessons I had learned from my mother's illness gave me an understanding of the human spirit that not many others could comprehend.

For most of my adult life, I felt as though when others met me, all they saw and experienced was a young girl with a lot to learn. They felt my fragmented, younger parts much more than the wise adult who was my mother's teacher. This was far from the truth of who I was. I did not know how to communicate or socialize in a way that allowed others to see my wisdom or my more mature parts. Perhaps the whole of me has never been able to be fully expressed, but I am confident that day will come.

Until recently, I didn't understand why my life always felt so hard. It was as if I had to work extra hard in every aspect of my life in order to compensate for something that was terribly lacking. Through Denise, I began to acknowledge how the trauma of my mother's mental illness forced my personality to fragment in order to protect itself.

Denise told me that DID can happen to children who are very bright and very creative. DID is sanity amid insanity. The fact that I was successfully becoming a higher-level student was a testament to the determination of my will to succeed and a testament to the personal, internal healing that had taken place.

Finding Her Here is a poem that Denise shared with me during this time. As I read it, I felt Denise's love and it touched me deeply and powerfully. Her acknowledgement of my personal growth was clearly communicated through the message of the poem and expressed her knowing of the woman I wished to become. Denise's trust in me, and her appreciation of our work together also shinned through. We had come a long way. The poem's author is unknown; the poem read as follows:

Finding Her Here

I am becoming the woman I've wanted, grey at the temples, soft body, delighted, cracked up by life with a laugh that's known bitter but, past it, got better, known she's a survivor—that whatever comes, she can outlast it. I am becoming a deep weathered basket.

I am becoming the woman I've longed for, the motherly lover with arms strong and tender, the growing up daughter who blushes surprises.

I am becoming full moons and sunrises. I find her becoming, this woman I've wanted, who knows she'll encompass, who knows she's sufficient, who knows where she's going and travels with passion. Who remembers she's precious, but knows she's not scarce—who knows she is plenty, plenty to share.

My first semester of physical therapy school was probably the hardest academic semester I had ever experienced. I was encouraged that I had survived round one. Before we began the physical therapy program, we were all advised of the strict academic requirements we needed to pass from one semester to the next. During the entire program, each student was allowed to make only two C's, and our overall GPA could not fall below 3.0. There was pressure academically, but when I was accepted into the program, I knew I would succeed. My marathon training taught me how to go the distance.

During my first semester, I learned a great deal and realized how appropriate my choice was in selecting physical therapy as my profession. I didn't know how much I enjoyed learning about the human body until I discovered how much there was to absorb. I could feel the excitement growing inside of me about how much I was going to gain in school. Eventually, I knew I would be able to be a teacher for my patients.

Academically, I had come a long way and had transformed myself from a person who was completely unable to focus in school to a student who was able to make A's in the classroom. I valued the opportunity to learn at a higher level and to learn from faculty who were part of a prestigious and respected program.

During my undergraduate days, I was never able to develop long-lasting relationships with my classmates or feel part of a class because my studies were spread out over the course of so many years. To be part of a program I could truly call my own at graduation meant the world to me.

Chapter 8

For the Life of a Mother

The Heart of Excellence

Mom when I was young, I knew your heart, but I did not know your dreams. When I was young, I knew your illness, and I knew your struggles, but I did not know your teacher. Today, I know your dreams because any illness that is so great can only define our greatest dreams; any dream that lives in your heart also lives in mine. Mom, today I know your teacher because any illness that is so great can only provide the greatest lessons; any lesson that lives in your heart also lives in mine.

When I was young, I knew my heart, and I knew my struggles, but I did not know my dreams. When I was young, I knew your illness, and I knew your violence, but I did not know your love. Today, Mom, I can feel your love, and I have discovered my dreams. Due to the teacher that I have discovered in you, Mom, I have discovered the teacher in me. Because of your dreams in me, I'm inspired to live the dream.

Mom, we have received greatly. I have discovered the excellence of my life's journey. Today, my heart knows that as I give to the world all that I have received from you—appreciation, love, humility and wisdom—somehow you too may awaken to the excellence of your life's journey.

This is the heart of excellence.

*A*t the same time I was beginning physical therapy training, I was still very much involved with my mother and her care and assisting her in different ways. She would frequently come to my grandmother's house or call me on the phone. In that way, our contact was continuous.

During the year leading up to my acceptance into Rockhurst, my mom had applied for—and was granted—medical disability due to her asthmatic condition. For years, my grandmother had pleaded with my mom to file for medical disability. However, my mom never wanted to be classified as mentally ill. As her respiratory status declined, the opportunity for my mom to receive medical disability became apparent.

This was significant for my grandmother and the rest of my family. No longer would my grandmother have to pay my mom's rent or provide the large sums of money needed in order to live her life. My grandmother was able to step back financially from assisting my mother, and she was able to regain some of her independence.

Once my mom began to receive medical disability, she became eligible for government-assisted housing and food stamps. The apartment where she was living was not Section-8-approved housing. Therefore she had to move to the Missouri side of Kansas City where Section 8 housing was available and she would have access to public transportation and the local grocery store. I was happy that my mom was finally receiving financial assistance because I understood how stressful life was for her relying on my grandmother for all of her needs. At the same time, I understood the stress my grandmother experienced as she felt the responsibility to provide for her daughter who was mentally and physically challenged. Our family was experiencing new beginnings in several ways.

When I think back, I recall years and years of family chaos and violence. Those years were traumatizing. However, the years that my mom spent living in Section 8 housing were some of the most stressful on a more personal and private level, which eventually led her to receive the mental help she had so desperately needed. My role in her life would be a critical piece if she were to maintain independent living moving forward.

When my mom initially moved into her apartment, she did a good job of maintaining her home and putting food on her table. For a person with schizophrenia and no medication, the simplest acts can be the greatest accomplishments. At times, I would see her out shopping, usually in an area of town that was serviced by public transportation. I was so happy that she had some independence, but I felt sad that she had to take the bus everywhere and had to carry her groceries for many blocks just to bring them home. Yet, even with this sadness in my heart, I always knew I wanted my mom to have the freedom to live her life as she wanted—just as any "normal" person is allowed to do.

I always encouraged her to do the things that other people were doing without feeling handicapped by her struggles. When I realized how hard life can be for someone who lives with mental illness, I gained a lot of respect and appreciation for the simple things in life that so many of us take for granted, and I realized how fortunate I was to be mentally healthy.

It was summertime, and I was running errands in the afternoon. I suddenly came upon my mom waiting at a bus stop. Within a second or two of seeing her, I could tell that she was tired from the heat and weighted down by the groceries she had just purchased. When my mom spotted me waving to her, she jumped up from the bench, gathered her groceries, and made a dash for my car. My timing was perfect.

As my mom got into my car, I could see there was a double-bagged bag of groceries, and it got my attention. It contained a half-gallon of ice cream, melting away. At that moment, I felt so much sadness in my heart. She needed my help getting her groceries home. Instantly, I felt the reality of my mother's mental illness and the hardship of her life. The simple pleasures in life that we take for granted can mean the world to someone with mental illness, like bringing home a half-gallon of ice cream without it melting. I have learned many lessons of humility in my life, and this was one of them.

To me, perhaps one of the most significant events in my mom's life, outside of her marriage to my father and the births of her four children, was when her years of living with schizophrenia without the aid of medication ended. For decades, everyone in the family had tried to provide her with the care she needed to address her illness. Until then, my mom's intelligence always stepped forward at just those times, negating any attempt by her family to treat her illness.

My mom's ability to take care of herself was declining. More and more, she displayed behaviors of a person who was severely mentally ill. She would isolate herself in her apartment; when I would call, there would be no answer—even though I knew she was home. She had stopped shopping for groceries and depended on my grandmother and me to purchase them for her.

When I delivered her groceries, she would take up to fifteen minutes sometimes to open her door in an apartment that was no bigger than five hundred square feet. I knew my mom was struggling. Physically, she was losing weight, and her teeth were beginning to fall out. When I visited, I began to notice roaches running across her kitchen table and the furniture in her small living room. On one occasion, I found a dead mouse in her bathtub. The most troubling thing was her lack of concern for the conditions in which she was living.

When she told me she was about to commit suicide, I had to take control. I had purchased some groceries and was delivering them to her. She was always so happy to see me when I came to visit because she knew I loved her with all of my heart and that I only wanted what was best for her. Based on our special bond, I knew her trust in me penetrated the walls that schizophrenia had created with everyone else in her life. I could hear her through her illness.

As I was putting her groceries away, she told me that she needed to talk with me. She began to tell me that the police had wired her apartment, and they were monitoring her from the outside. She went on to tell me that a voice in her head had told her to cut an artery. At that moment, I understood my mom was telling me that she had a battle raging inside, and she needed help. I never shared my mom's words with anyone in my family. However, I understood the seriousness of what was present for her.

While my mom was declining, my grandmother, one of my brothers, and I had been actively seeking the assistance of a caseworker in Missouri to help us take guardianship of her. If a person is known to be a danger to him or herself, a court warrant could be issued to have the person picked up, against his or her will, and placed in a mental health facility for at least forty-eight hours for observation.

Furthermore, if during that time, the treating psychiatrist determined that the person was mentally incapacitated, that information could be used in court to award guardianship to a willing and able family member. It was clear that my mom was no longer able to live safely without intervention.

My grandmother was getting older, and my youngest brother was intensively involved with his family practice residency. Even though I had just started physical therapy school, I knew I needed to be the one to step forward to become my mother's guardian in order to save her life.

With the aid of the caseworker, a court-appointed warrant was issued for my mom. The caseworker and I arranged with the local police a day and time to stage an intervention to have my mom placed in the state mental facility for observation and evaluation. On the day of the intervention, I called my mom and told her that she was very sick and that she had to get the help she so desperately needed. I told her not to be scared and that I was coming to her apartment and was going to escort her to the hospital. I told her that I had to bring the police because they were going to make sure she made it safely to the hospital. I was scared. I was sad. I knew I needed to be stronger than at any point in my life. I could feel what was about to happen.

My mom lived on the ninth floor; when I saw the police car pull up to my mom's apartment building, I knew the situation was real. I was sad for the trauma my mom was about to experience, but I trusted that I was doing the right thing. There were two police officers in the squad car, but only one got out. We took the elevator to my mom's apartment.

I knocked and said, "Mom, it is Kelly. I'm here to help you go to the hospital. I have a police officer with me to help us."

It was one of the hardest days of my life. I had to be steadfast in my desire to help her get out of the hell she was living in.

Reluctantly, my mom opened the door. As soon as she did, we moved quickly into her apartment. We asked her to please go with us to the hospital willingly. We told her we were there to help her get the help she needed. Without hesitation, the police officer and I took hold of my mom's arms and began to escort her down the hall to the waiting elevator.

As we did, she began to scream to her neighbors for help. She screamed that she was being taken away against her will. One of her neighbors opened her door, and my mom begged her to stop us. It took everything in me not to cry. One of my main concerns was that my mom would have an asthma attack during the intervention. It was common when she was stressed to have an asthma attack, but the intervention went smoothly.

We made it out to the police car, and I sat in the back seat with her during our drive to the hospital. I tried to reassure her that everything was going to be okay. I knew her worst nightmare had just come true, that the police had been monitoring her, and now they had come to get her. I told her that she would be feeling better soon.

Once we reached the hospital, my mom and I were taken into a private room where we spoke with several of the staff members and a physician. I felt uneasy as they began to ask her questions. They asked her to empty her purse; when she refused, the doctor dumped her belongings out on the table. I felt the humiliation my mom felt. It was obvious that these people were used to dealing with the mentally ill in a way I would never again choose for my mom. She began screaming that she was not a prisoner and had rights. She became hysterical, and I was afraid for her safety. I wanted to stop the process and remind the people that they were dealing with a human being.

Even though she was mentally ill, she was a decent, intelligent woman. The stress of the situation was so high that I began to cry. I couldn't help myself, even though I fought hard to keep my emotions under control. I asked my mom to please do what they asked—to please cooperate. I assured her that they were not there to hurt her. When I became emotional, she calmed down. From that point on, she was relatively cooperative.

My mom's stay at the state hospital was successful. Every day she was there, I prayed that the universe would protect her from harm. There were many interesting characters at the state hospital, but I knew in my heart that she was at the right place and that her time there would be short and effective. It became clear to the medical personnel that my mom was mentally ill but very intelligent. With the aid of the hospital psychiatrist, and the support of my brother and the rest of my family, I was successful in gaining guardianship during her stay by participating in a court hearing on her behalf.

Within two weeks, my mom was discharged and placed in a nursing home. I was thankful for the success of my mom's hospitalization and felt hopeful for her future. Finally, after decades of living with untreated schizophrenia, my mom had medication for her illness. Yet, the struggle that we had with her for years to get her to comply with taking medication again became an issue soon after she moved into the nursing home.

Initially, I was concerned about her moving. Its location was very close to the apartment building where she had just been living, and it wasn't too far from the bus line. I knew she had made good strides while being a patient at the state hospital, but I also knew my mom's initial recovery was very fragile and would probably not last long. I alerted the staff at the nursing home to be aware of her history of leaving and her medication non-compliance. The nursing home was full of patients with an array of physical and mental illnesses. I knew it would be a challenge for them to keep up with my mom.

Within two weeks, I began receiving phone calls that my mom was non-compliant with her medications and staying on the property. As it turned out, she was boarding a bus at the closest bus stop and taking day trips around the city. She was also asking strangers for rides when she didn't have money for the bus fare. Again, I was concerned for her safety. I knew I needed to make a change in her facility and find one in another part of town. I decided to transition her care to Kansas.

The fact that my family and I were actively involved with my mom's care—and that I had successfully become my mom's guardian—played a huge role in the quality of care that she was able to receive. I knew she had once again become mentally unstable. All the gains we had made at the state hospital were beginning to unravel. I knew she needed to be stabilized on medication before I could even think about finding a new long-term facility. She needed to be hospitalized again. This time, she was placed in a facility far away from her old neighborhood, which provided a more gentle approach to mental health. I felt the assistance of the universe collaborating with my family and me to help my mom.

Within a week or so of hospitalization, she was showing signs of stabilizing. I began to talk with social services about long-term care for her. We discussed her need to live in a new neighborhood where she wouldn't have access to a bus line or neighbors who would give her rides if she asked.

As it turned out, there was an opening in a nursing home in a wonderful little town about thirty minutes from the hospital. The nursing home provided transportation to a local mental health facility that offered day programs and case management in an effort to help the patients re-establish independence. The only requirement was that I had to have my mom's Missouri disability funds transferred to Kansas. I began the process.

My mom stayed in the hospital for about three weeks. As she stabilized on medication, she began to build a more solid foundation for normal living. The day she transitioned from the hospital to the nursing home, I felt excited for the opportunity that was in front of her. I was heavy with sadness to see her become a resident of a facility that housed so many people who were completely mentally and physically incapacitated. While she was opposed to living in a nursing home, I assured her that my goal, along with the rest of the family, was to help her regain her independence, but it was up to her.

After living there for three years, she successfully transitioned to independent living. During those years, I spent a lot of time with her, mostly taking her out of the facility so she could enjoy some normal aspects of living. I was determined to protect my mom from becoming institutionalized, as is so often the case for persons living in long-term care facilities. I was also able to develop a relationship with her that I had never had before, one that wasn't so colored by schizophrenia.

At times, I began to feel as though I had a mom. Once she stabilized on medication, she began attending a day program at the nearby mental health facility. Once there, she was assigned a caseworker that eventually, helped guide her back to independent living.

The program turned out to be the inspiration and intervention she needed to turn her life around. With the help of medication and structure, my mom realized that the rest of her life could be spent in a nursing home or she could take advantage of what was being offered. If she wanted to, she could become a productive citizen through the help of the day program. It truly was up to her.

As I look back, I realize the time that my mom spent in the nursing home turned out to be some her more productive years. Perhaps the greatest gifts that the nursing home and day program provided were the opportunity to become employed again. It had been years since she had been able to hold down a job.

With the help of her caseworker, she began to perform odd jobs at the mental health facility. It became evident that my mom was able to thrive when she could give herself to something and make it her own. As she continued to show signs of higher-level functioning, the mental health facility decided to employ my mom part-time to manage a small library.

"Audrey's Alcove" was born, and my mom's purpose in life was renewed. I was happy for my mom's success and grateful for the people who had helped her along her way. For many with mental illness, just getting out of bed in the morning and grooming themselves is quite a task. To this day, my mom tells me to be thankful that I have a job.

When it became evident that my mom might be capable of moving out of the nursing home and into an apartment for independent living, there was concern within my family about the appropriateness of this decision. I knew that my mom deserved a chance to show what she was capable of at this point in her life. If she were to never get the opportunity, we would truly be limiting her.

In November 2001, my mom regained her independence and moved into her own apartment in the same small town where the nursing home was located. My family and I took a lot of comfort knowing that if she were not to succeed on her own, the nursing home was literally just down the street. Her road to independence would not be easy, but I knew she would rather live on her own and struggle than be held captive in an environment she had successfully outgrown. She had earned this chance.

As my mom transitioned to independent living, she continued to attend the day program at the mental health facility and showed good signs of higher-level functioning for several years thereafter. Then her compliance with medication again became an issue. Gradually, she required more assistance living independently.

On June 17, 2009, my mom was hospitalized for exacerbation of her asthmatic condition. This began her transition into assisted living, where she now resides comfortably and with great care. Her transition into assisted living would not have been possible without the help of my mom's sisters, the State of Kansas, and the help of a wonderful woman from a professional nursing organization.

One of the great gifts to come from my mother's schizophrenia was my opportunity to become a person of depth, love, and understanding. Another gift came from my guardianship of my mom. Our relationship focused on health and success rather than illness, violence, and destruction.

As I worked with Denise, I became stronger. My foundation was healthier, and I was able to guide my mom to the assistance that she needed in a way that was respectful for both of us. In this way, I was able to give to myself the mother I had always wanted.

With time, I was able to talk with my mom about life and about our dreams. We were able to do the things that other people do; we went out to eat, went to the movies, and even attended a show in Las Vegas. The fact that my mom was able to board a plane and travel was a testament to her recovery. Recently, she was able to attend her seventieth birthday party with several of our family members present.

What a gift! The recovery that my grandmother so adamantly sought for my mom was now a reality! While full "recovery" from schizophrenia is not possible for my mom at this point in her life, her ability to live a peaceful and meaningful life with the aide of medication, structure and family assistance is incredibly successful for her and for our entire family.

Throughout this process, I continued my physical therapy program and my work with Denise. I am certain those two stabilizing and life-giving forces were paramount in my ability to come forward to help my mom. My studies required me to focus intensively, and my work with

Denise provided a foundation of love and respect for my future and for me.

My mom knew that my studies were of utmost importance, and she held high regard for my desire to further my life through education. She was also aware of the deep relationship that I had developed with Denise. I believe my mom appreciated Denise for her ability to step into my life and offer much of what she was not able to provide.

My work with my mom left me humble on most days, but my work with furthering my education allowed me to build passion and excitement for my future. In school, I found myself building self-esteem and self-confidence through the required coursework and student presentations. While I did not feel as though I had a lot of friends in the program, I felt as though I had gained the respect of my classmates. I was learning how to become a teacher for the patients I would eventually treat, and I was becoming a teacher for myself.

During the second semester of my therapy program, while I was being tested to the utmost with my desire to help my mom, to complete the grueling coursework, and to become the person I knew that I could become, I was given one of the greatest gifts in my life. The spark I needed to go the distance arrived. Ever since then, I have walked the earth a better person, an inspired person, a person who is determined to raise my level of existence to world-class excellence.

Chapter 9

The Power of the Dream

Touching One Heart to Another, the Gift of Music

Although our father was never a part of our lives, the musician who lived within him is a significant part of who my siblings and I have become. The musician who lived within his heart is the gift that allowed our father to be a part of our lives, although we never knew him. It was the tie that brought our hearts together in the safest way possible. Had it not been for our grandparents nurturing our musical talents, perhaps the greatest gift to come from our childhood would not have been possible.

The "Holland Four" was a safe port in the storm. With music, we did not know mental illness or the absence of a father. With music, our childhood was a gift from God, and we were able to live with the self-esteem and confidence that we had never known. When singing, we were able to show the world what was possible when given a chance. With music, we were able to share a common bond that was healthy and loving. We were united in our hearts, then and now.

On March 29, 1999, I attended a concert and realized one more teacher had entered my life. This teacher was different. She was a teacher from a distance, yet her impact on my life was profound. The father of a dear man I was dating invited both of us to see a Celine Dion concert. I had heard of Celine's music, but I had never seen her perform live in concert. I was very excited and felt in my heart that it was going to be a special night.

The night started off rather interestingly. Six of us crammed into a small car for the thirty-minute drive to the arena. We laughed and played as we made our way to the show. I could already feel the influence of Celine and was excited to be a part of the evening.

The show was sold out, and there was electricity in the air. It wasn't five minutes into the start of the show when I realized that my life had changed. For the first time, I felt the heart of a champion. I heard the voice of a God-given talent like no other. I knew I was experiencing the Michael Jordan of music, and I was witnessing the work ethic that defines excellence.

On that night, I was inspired to raise my level of existence to world-class excellence. A desire was born within me to meet Celine. The power of this dream would become a mighty force in my life for years to come.

I left the arena that night on fire. I had witnessed a greatness that has changed me forever. The next morning, I was a different person. Internally, I had changed. The energy in which Celine performed her show now lived within me. The sadness of so many years had lifted. I felt electric. I was truly energized for what was possible in my life. I felt excitement about my future. I knew that the gift of Celine's concert was not a coincidence.

The universe was showing me a side of life that I had never experienced before—the power to become my best. During my drive to school the next morning, I heard a DJ talking on the radio about Celine's concert. He, too, had been mesmerized by her show. I walked into school that day wearing a headset, listening to Celine's music. I had passion in my heart, and I began to dream of what was possible. Through Celine's music, I could feel the power within me like never before, and nothing was going to bring me down.

The energy and passion with which Celine delivered her music were like no other. Through her songs, Celine's heart beats loudly. Yet, perhaps her greatest gift is her ability to connect with her audience in a way that allows the best of her to bond with the best in them. This is a primary gift—inspiring the best in others by offering only your best to them.

Since that first concert, I have seen Celine perform many times. Each time, I walk away a better person, inspired to become my best, and with the desire to talk with the world about what is possible when you have passion in your heart and believe in your dreams. When you believe, the universe will show you a path to greatness.

Soon after I saw Celine perform in 1999, I learned that she performed that night after recently learning that her husband Rene' had been diagnosed with cancer. Yet, during her show, I only saw excellence. She was fully present. Her focus was impeccable! Then in December of 2009, when I saw her in Phoenix, Arizona, her performance again was the best I had ever seen. Later, I learned that she had been very sick leading up to the show and had considered canceling her performance. But I only saw excellence.

What speaks loudest to me is the person behind the music. Celine's determination to be her best without exception and her ability to demand the best from others define her excellence.

She is a role model of love and stability in an industry that destroys many. And although she is one of the most successful singers in the world, she remains humble and appreciates her audience for "giving her the opportunity to perform." I'm grateful for her willingness to live her life as an open book. In a world where fear runs rampant, she sets an example of what love and trust can create when given a chance—a loving relationship that benefits many.

Having discovered Celine's talent and her incredible work ethic, I now understand world-class excellence. I understand that to be considered world-class, every word you choose to speak, whether in silence to yourself, to a family member, or to a stranger on the street, determines what you present to the world. After every show I've attended, I feel her greatness beating in the hearts of those who came to see her. That's when you know that you have a made a difference.

I recognize and appreciate with all of my being the excellence that Denise has taught me, and the excellence that I found in my relationship with my mother and my family. Through Celine, my world expanded. Over time, as these three teachers have come together in my life, I know with every fiber of my being the perfection of the universe. I now understand that the universe is a masterful mind and assists us in living our greatest lives, but only if we are willing to appreciate the opportunities presented by all the teachers in our lives.

Today, I stand inspired by my life's teachers, to light up the world by sharing my message of inspiration and excellence that has become my own. I stand inspired to ignite the spirit of the world through my passion and to demonstrate that no matter where you are in life—emotionally, mentally, in health, or financially—all dreams are possible when you believe. Belief is where all dreams begin. To have a dream is where life begins. It is a call from the heart, the spirit—to connect the greatest source of man with the greater source, the universe. It is your inner genius leading the way, guiding you to align with your truest self.

Through the teachings of Abraham and Jerry and Esther Hicks, I understand how our beliefs shape our lives. According to their teachings, every thought that you think produces a feeling or emotion within you. And every emotion produces a specific vibration or a frequency that emanates from you and interacts with the universe. And as your vibration interacts with the universe, the universe responds by sending back to you manifestations that match the vibration that you offer. Simply speaking, a positive person emits a positive vibration that attracts other positive people or vice versa. The expressions, "birds of a feather flock together" or "misery loves company", communicates precisely this powerful, universal law of attraction. It is real. It is as real as the gravity that keeps us on our planet, as Abraham claims.

Similarly, you communicate your life's desires to the universe through your thoughts and feelings. And, it is your vibration that matters most! Your vibration is honest. It "speaks" your truth! Vibration is your heart's communication and your truest tie to the universe. Too believe in your life's dreams, truly, communicates to the universe an intention to live your dreams. When believing, you radiate a signal or frequency of expectation for what is to unfold in your life and the universe responds. Our beliefs are what set us apart. When you believe, you receive assistance of the highest order, the support of the universe. There is nothing more powerful.

To believe in your dream is to allow the journey to unfold—to allow the universe to tend to your dream. The journey takes center stage. It is how you evolve, and it gives your life meaning. It is how appreciation finds your heart. To want something and then to receive it is to feel great joy in life, which allows your heart to sing with beautiful music. To want something and then to receive it is to discover the powerful person who lives within you—a true gift within your dreams. To allow your journey to unfold is to communicate trust in the universe that your dreams have been heard. It is trusting in your ability to receive. This is the art of allowing.

Perhaps there is no greater dream than becoming a parent. Perhaps there is no greater, more challenging journey than parenthood. Perhaps there is no greater feeling than being a parent and witnessing your children living their dreams. To watch others live their dreams, we then feel the greatness of the human spirit and the generosity that lives within each of us. It is the highest standard of giving, rather than receiving.

When you have a dream that lives within your heart, it becomes a part of who you are. It goes everywhere with you—in your feelings, your thoughts, your decisions, and your actions. When you tend to it everyday, through your focused love and energy, it becomes your guiding light. It leads your way. It is what gets you out of bed in the morning and lifts your spirits when you have a difficult day. It is what fills your heart with hope. If you didn't dream of what could be, you would never work to become because your will is found in your dreams. Soon, your dreams will lead you to have other dreams. And then, the life that you create will be better than any life you have ever imagined. This is the power of the dream. It is the power that unites your life.

Perhaps there is no greater stage than the Olympics, where dreams begin and where dreams are realized. To dream as a child, to live as your Olympic hero, and then to accomplish as an adult—this is the power of the dream. To dream as a team, to win a gold medal for your country, to dream as a nation, to stand with great accomplishment in the eyes of world—this is the power of the dream. To stand as an Olympic champion on the worlds' largest stage calls many to their greatest selves. To train and compete relentlessly for years, pushing the limits of what is physically possible, to then discover the excellence that lives within, in strength, endurance, confidence, and courage. Our dreams never tire. The source of our dreams is the energy of life itself, the universe, and eternal consciousness. The power of the dream lives within each of us, standing as champions in our own lives, so that we too may discover our own heroes within.

Recently, I watched an interview with Olympian and three-time gold medalist, Kerri Walsh Jennings and her mom, Margie Walsh. The interview, *Raising an Olympian,* was a commercial sponsored by Proctor and Gamble. It was powerful, and the message was clear. Role models make a difference in shaping who we become. But to stand as an Olympic athlete, you must first stand as an Olympian in life. For Kerri, her mom was the difference, her rock, and her stabilizing force. From her, Kerri learned to dream big and to believe in herself. She learned how to be relentless, to be a winner, and how to never settle for anything but the best from herself and from life. Kerri spoke of her mom's love, repeatedly, and of how she, too, learned how to love. She spoke of how her mom's spirit was tough and bright. Margie spoke of the person who Kerri had become. This is what she was most proud of, more than Kerri becoming an Olympian.

After the United States won the gold medal in men's basketball, head basketball coach Mike Krzyzewski said his players' mindset of cooperation and trust in each other, in him, and in his coaching staff, and the opportunity to represent the United States, were key factors that led to the team's success. He spoke of the true greatness of the team and their ability to put aside their egos and come together as a team so the country they represented could stand proud in the end.

Coach Krzyzewski's ability to bring together the best basketball talent in the world and unite them as a winning team conveys a world-class level of leadership. He demonstrates respect for the men that he coaches and respect for the game. He demonstrates that winning begins at the top. Mike Krzyzewski is also the head basketball coach at Duke University.

His influence in the game is legendary. His winning percentage is among the highest in sports history. Coach 'K' is an Olympian in life and is a true Olympic hero.

To discover a life's hero is where dreams begin. One of life's amazing gifts is seeing the greatness in another purely, innocently, and without flaws. It is a gift for the heart. It is a gift from the heart—of appreciation and love. To find a life's hero is to find a teacher, whether from the schoolhouse or the firehouse, from Hollywood or your neighborhood. Our teachers stand powerfully and shape our lives. To find a life's hero is to stand in awe of what already lives within you. It is to outwardly see what is inwardly cherished, a reflection of your own heart.

Through admiration, you are called to what matters. You begin to dream of what is possible in your own life. You take notice of where you stand. You begin to look for ways to close the gap. For some, it is a lifelong journey. It is a journey of complete transformation, a journey that drops you to your knees to allow you to then stand on the mountaintop. For others, closing the gap is merely allowing your dreams to fall into your life.

Heroes come forward and touch our lives, through deed or inspiration, and from all walks of life. What we choose to do with their influence is up to us. Your hero will take you as far as your heart and determination allows.

In the summer of 1996, the world came together for the opening ceremonies of the Olympic Game's in Atlanta, Georgia. Celine sang "The Power of the Dream" and touched the heart of the world through her talent, grace, passion, and inspiration. "The Power of the Dream", inspired the world to stand tall, be its best in the light of the Olympic flame, and cheer for our heroes to realize their dreams. On this night, I was inspired too, but it wasn't until three years later that my spirit would ignite.

Celine's concert in Kansas City in 1999 was in perfect order. The momentum of my life was such that I could hear the call; my work with Denise had allowed it. Something greater than physical therapy was now alive within me. Through Celine and her incredible stage presence, my true self awakened. No longer could I feel the heaviness of my life. I had found a new level. On that night, I launched into orbit the desire and the energy to create my best life. Overnight, Celine had become one of my life's heroes. She changed the course of my life, and I learned how to really dream. I began to think of myself in a greater way, a more powerful way, expanding my life into something much greater than myself. I began to dream of talking to the world and sharing what had come alive in my heart. I could feel the energy that creates the worlds that Abraham and Jerry and Esther Hicks speaks of. I could feel the energy of a life worth living. I could feel the energy of inspiring others.

Today, I am a different person. I am a person of immense passion, electricity, creativity, and knowledge. I have searched through the universe to find my best self, and today I am closing the gap. I have traveled far. I know that having a life's hero is one of life's greatest gifts. It is to receive the light of life. It is to take the best of your life's hero and make it your own. This is a process. It's a journey. This is the power within our dreams. Currently, my dream is to inspire those who have inspired me. Today, my dream is to keep dreaming. Thinking of my dreams leaves me feeling good. It serves me well, and my inner world benefits. From good thoughts come good feelings, and good things happen when you feel good.

From Abraham and Jerry and Esther Hicks, I have learned why our dreams matter. As stated previously, every thought carries a vibration, a signal, and an emotional feeling. When we dream, we focus on what we want. A positive focus leaves us feeling happy. Happiness is then our vibrational interaction with the universe. And the universe responds by sending more of the same. From our happiness, we create an emotional environment where we can further create. It is the practice of deliberate creation. To have a dream is to train your mind how to focus. To dream is to teach you how to feel good. To dream is to teach yourself how to focus on what feels good until you realize that feeling good is what dreams are made of.

In simple terms, planning a vacation is having a dream. It is to think positively of what the future holds. It is to ignore the specifics of life and what doesn't feel good, and to then focus on your vacation and what does feel good. When you go on a vacation, life seems easier. Mentally you can handle more. Your mind is more creative, and your heart is more loving. You have greater energy, and you feel appreciation. You require less sleep. Oftentimes, you eat less. Things that usually bother you bounce off; you are impermeable to matters that don't feel good. Your good-feeling state dominates. It is a protective shield. In time, others notice your good mood, and they want to be around you more. Your positive energy is infectious. It spreads. Internally, through your emotion and vibration, you have created an environment that attracts success, just from focusing on your future vacation.

Your dreams are the same. When you dream, you step out of reality and the specifics of your life and into the generalness of your good-feeling dream. You take a break internally from the stress of life. You feel non-resistant for a moment. In thought, you create your future success, your dream. You feel good. When you emerge from dreaming, you carry the positive vibration with you. You are living in the energy of your dreams. Your future success becomes your current success. The more you dream, the better you feel—until your dream is your current reality. This is the power of your dreams!

Through Abraham, I better understand the laws of the universe, the law of attraction, deliberate creation, and the art of allowing. I understand this powerful role of the universe in assisting me in living my dreams. These laws give hope to those who trust their existence. These laws give hope to those who dare to dream. They have allowed me to know that what I give my focus and attention to for a mere seventeen seconds or greater, is enough time to begin the creation process of what I have focused upon. "It is law," says Abraham. I have also learned that, at times, we are truly not aware of the power that lives within us to create until the evidence of our power is fully displayed.

One morning, I was meditating on my balcony, quietly listening to nature and visualizing the events of my past few days. I had just returned from Celine's show in Las Vegas. I was in a good place emotionally. As I meditated, my thoughts began to wander. I could see Celine performing her show. I watched as she twirled a baton in the air while performing one of her songs. As my meditation continued, suddenly my focus turned negative. I envisioned the baton leaving Celine's hand and hitting my nose. My seat was only a few rows from the stage. I fell to the ground, and my nose began to bleed. I was in pain. As I sat on my balcony experiencing this meditation, I began to cry. I could feel the power of this all-encompassing vision I had created. I opened my eyes.

Just then, a wasp flew by my head and into my house. I began to feel nervous. As a child and as an adult I had been stung, and my fear of bees and wasps has escalated. As I tracked the wasp into my house, it began to fly toward my head. I ducked and turned to run. As I did, I hit my nose on the arm of a wrought iron chair and fell to the floor. I had broken my nose. I was in extreme pain, and I could tell that I had sustained a concussion. I was in shock.

As I was lying on the floor, I was aware that I had just created the contents of my meditation while sitting on the balcony. Over and over, I could hear a voice in my head telling me never again to question the power of my focus. Never! Yet, I soon started to realize the massive gift I had just received. I knew that the years I had spent visualizing my dreams was well spent. I had come to realize that if I could create this event in my life so quickly, then I embodied the power to create anything in my life that I gave my attention to. What a wake-up call.

I stayed on the floor for twenty minutes, recovering. My legs were weak, and the pain in my head was off the pain scale. The power of this event ran through me like a lightning bolt striking a tree. I knew that the universe had spoken. I was listening. I was to sharpen my focus and deliberately focus on the positive, only giving my attention to what I want to bring into my life, period. Eventually, I made it back to my feet, cautiously. The wasp was nowhere in sight. The message had been delivered. I spent the rest of that day icing and resting. I wasn't able to do much. The next week, I was traumatized. Physically I was fragile, but my focus was sharp. I began to experience laser focus. No longer did I allow my mind to wander into unpleasant and unwanted matters. I had learned a powerful lesson and had received a gift of a lifetime: the power of my focus and trust in my ability to create.

This life event was real. It has changed me. I feel somewhat embarrassed when sharing this story; however, I do so to assist others to live a powerful, positive life. I know that I am no different than any other human being on this planet. We all embody the same power to focus if the body and mind are intact. If I can create in my life the contents of my thoughts so quickly, so can you. I also understand that bigger dreams require more time, more sustained focus. It is that simple.

I am learning how to shift my focus more quickly away from the unwanted and toward things I desire for my life. It is a process. I knew previously that the dream to meet Celine had given me the gift of focus for my life. I have a new level of focus today. The universe knew that I needed an intervention to sharpen my focus. Creating and living big dreams requires big-time focus, never losing the vision. The relentless pursuit of the dream through relentless positive focus will allow your dreams to unfold at just the right time and at just the right place.

Thank you, Celine. From you, the power of the dream came to life!

Chapter 10

Excellence in Motion

When All Is Still,
Here Am I — Lovingly

For many years, I internalized the stress that lived within my mother and, in turn, I internalized her struggle. For years, I used drugs to live. I had become detached from the loving, knowing child who once was me. I did not know love for myself or for anyone. In my mind, I was broken into pieces, and my body was at war.

At fifty, I have returned to the loving, peaceful being who I came here to be. When I sit quietly, and all is still, lovingly, I see the person I've become. Today, I understand the turmoil that creates a mind that cannot focus or a body that cannot rest. I understand how great pain is created in our bodies.

Today, I fully understand the mind-body connection. That is why I became a physical therapist—to help others heal.

I couldn't help noticing the timing of the gift when I was able to attend Celine's concert. It came when I was taking control of my mother's life and becoming her legal guardian. It was as if the universe was showing me that no matter how challenging it was assisting my mother, my focus was to be on creating my best life and living my passion.

I returned to Rockhurst for my second year of physical therapy school in the fall of 1999. I had heard through the grapevine that if I was going to make it through physical therapy school, surviving the first semester of the second year was going to be my greatest challenge. Never before had I taken twenty-one hours in a given semester, but I believed that by being accepted into this program the universe was showing me that I had what it takes to be successful. At the same time, Celine announced that she was going to perform in Montreal, Canada, on New Year's Eve to ring in the new century.

The thought of traveling to Montreal to attend Celine's show was just the motivation that I needed to successfully complete the hardest semester. Celine's concert was going to be a gift in my life. Only this time, it was a gift to myself for a job well done. The call to raise my level of existence to world-class excellence inspired me in every phase of my life.

Perhaps one of the great discoveries to come out of my education was identifying the reason that I had struggled academically for so many years. The Americans with Disabilities Act, which ensures that accommodations are provided for all people with disabilities, allowed me to successfully become the medical professional I am today. Since childhood, my ability to read was limited. My greatest challenge was not reading the word itself but remembering what I had read and being able to comprehend the meaning of what I was reading.

Mostly, I was unable to sustain my focus or my attention long enough to successfully interpret what I was reading. Often, I had to read the same paragraph three or four times or even more to fully understand what was being communicated. In the seventh grade, I was put into a special reading class that was to assist me in learning how to read faster and to improve my reading comprehension. That did not happen. As I grew, I found myself avoiding classes that required a lot of reading. I knew that I was missing out on a lot of my education, but my difficulties with reading affected my academic decisions.

When I considered a career in physical therapy, I investigated physical therapy programs across the country. I learned that many of them required applicants to complete the Graduate Entrance Examination. The GRE focused largely on reading comprehension. I decided to take a preparatory course prior to taking the GRE to familiarize myself with the material and to hopefully improve my score.

As it turned out, my initial score was so low that I knew that I didn't stand a chance of being accepted into physical therapy school. Denise and I had talked about my inability to focus for any length of time. Denise believed that my struggles with reading were due to a condition known as Attention Deficit and Hyperactivity Disorder (ADHD). It all began to make sense as I looked back on my early years at Kansas University. When I began my college career, I took fifteen to eighteen hours of classes each semester. Quickly, I was overwhelmed by the amount of material I had to learn. And given that I was struggling with a drug addition, I was positioned to fail. Later, when I resumed my studies, I took classes part-time. In that way, I was able to learn at a much slower pace, and I was able to succeed. I accommodated my disability.

With Denise's help, I submitted a letter to the examination board requesting additional time to take the GRE exam. Denise figured that I would require double the allotted time. I struggled with the idea of asking for additional time. Denise explained that those persons who have ADHD and who are allotted extra time to take their exams have improved scores. For persons who do not have ADHD, the additional time made no difference in their scores. When I retook the GRE with the extended time, my scores improved by four hundred points!

As it turned out, Rockhurst University did not require applicants to sit for the GRE. Nonetheless, the fact that I had requested additional testing time from the board of examiners who administered the GRE helped to further pave the way for me academically. By doing so, I continued to receive the testing accommodations that allowed me to be successful in my physical therapy program and beyond.

During physical therapy school, I struggled with the realization that I had to ask for extra time on exams. I wanted to be just like any other student in my classes. I didn't want to feel as though I was being singled out or that I was receiving special treatment because something was wrong with me. I wanted to be respected for who I was as a person rather than to be seen as a student with a disability. I believe if each person on earth had to live one day with a physical disability for all to see, there would be no more judgment of our differences. Through my relationship with my mom, I have learned that it only takes one person to treat another with respect before others will follow.

I share this to serve as an inspiration for those who may think that a disability will keep them from realizing their dreams. As I have learned, when you have passion in your heart to make your dreams become your reality, the universe will provide a path for your dreams to unfold.

To begin, you must believe and trust in your power and ability to live your dream rather than believing in the limitations of your disability. As a student with ADHD, I learned that by receiving additional time on my exams, I was only leveling the playing field so that I could have the same opportunity as my classmates. On a final note, as I progressed, two other students in my class were granted extra time on exams. By the end of our program, I did not sit alone!

As I look back on my three years of physical therapy school, I am indebted to Rockhurst University and the faculty who assisted me in my efforts to become a physical therapist. From day one, they welcomed me with open arms and provided, without hesitation, the accommodations that I needed in order to successfully complete the program. Academically, Rockhurst University sits at the top. And I found it to be an institution of integrity and class. I grew enormously as a student and as a person at Rockhurst. At the end of each academic year, every student was required to pass an exam that covered material from the entire year. By doing so, we demonstrated that we were ready to progress to the next level. They were also preparing us to pass the national boards required once graduation was completed. What I learned at Rockhurst is that they are not only interested in you successfully completing the program but in becoming a standout professional.

Completing my degree was the hardest educational experience of my life to that point. On Sunday, May 11, 2001, Mother's Day, I walked across the stage at Rockhurst University and received my master's degree in physical therapy. For the first time, I felt as though I had brought to my family and myself a sense of pride and accomplishment that only a few years ago would not have been possible.

I had wanted to be part of a graduating class that I could call my own, and finally the day had come. I wanted to show my family the person who lived inside of me. One of my most memorable moments was when I attended my hooding ceremony the day before graduation, and I saw Denise in the audience. Finally, I was able to share the success of our journey and show her the power of our relationship. Denise's presence in my life was one of the biggest reasons that day had come.

I passed the national boards and officially became a licensed physical therapist in August of 2001. I had been working part-time in the admitting office at St. Luke's Hospital in Kansas City, Missouri. In all, I had been an employee at St. Luke's for twelve years before becoming a licensed physical therapist.

As I look back, I'm thankful for the stability the hospital provided during a time when I was turning my life around and completing my education. I felt proud to be an employee of such a respected hospital, and I was eager to continue my employment there as a physical therapist. As it turned out, after interviewing for the position, I was offered a full-time physical therapy job, and my transition into the therapy department was seamless. I could feel in my heart that I had turned the corner in my life professionally, and I was excited to apply all the knowledge that I had gained during my three years of graduate school.

My initial job was to float between inpatient and outpatient services. This was a perfect fit for me since I wanted to learn the many different aspects of the profession. As it turned out, after only three months working on the main hospital campus, I was transferred to the Northland Hospital, and that was where I finished my employment at St. Luke's.

One of the most important decisions I made regarding my life as a professional came right before I graduated. As my education was winding down, I sensed that although I had been successful with completing all of the coursework required to graduate, I was struggling clinically. I knew I wanted to offer 'excellence in motion' for my patients. I wanted them to receive world-class care. I wanted them to know the excellence that lived within me and within them! Yet the pace at which I was required to learn left me feeling as though I had to step back and review matters before I could fully move ahead. I knew my struggles with ADHD had created a clinical gap for me, and I was aware that I needed to go the extra mile in order to become an effective therapist.

I decided to ask one of my third-year instructors if I could do an extra clinical rotation with him after I had graduated. That decision affected the direction of my career because of the excellence I witnessed from another teacher who had entered my life. It began during our final semester of school. We were allowed to take course electives to customize our educations. Through the grapevine, I had heard that one instructor was very passionate about the subject he taught. Students who had taken his course did well when they entered the real world. He was a spine physical therapist, and he was well known in the community for his skills. He had created his own teaching company in which he offered continuing education courses for other therapists and served as adjunct faculty at Rockhurst.

It wasn't long into the semester before I realized I wanted to pattern my career after his. I wanted to become a spine physical therapist and become a teacher within the profession. Through his passion, I learned a great deal about the spine. If I could treat the spine effectively, there was no other muscular-skeletal pathology that I would not be able to treat.

To this day, I appreciate the impact he made on the direction of my career. He helped make me the professional that I am. My life changed that summer when he asked me to join his teaching company once I had completed my extra clinical rotation. It was a chance of a lifetime, especially for a new graduate who had yet to treat a patient. Even though I was very green professionally, he knew that if I was willing to perform an extra clinical rotation to better myself clinically, then I would be willing to go the extra mile to help his company succeed.

I assisted with his teaching company for two years before I decided to leave my hometown to pursue my life's passions elsewhere. I had come to a point in my life personally and professionally where I felt a great change was needed. Professionally, I was beginning to feel a sense of independence as a clinician, and I had an urge to find a place of employment that would allow my talents as a physical therapist to be fully utilized.

I continued to serve as my mother's legal guardian. She was stable with the help of the mental health center and her case manager. For the very first time, I felt the desire and freedom to pursue my life outside of Kansas City. The only thing that would keep me there was my relationship with Denise. But as it turned out, Denise was my biggest fan for beginning my new life somewhere else.

My transition out of Kansas City began during the fall of 2003. I had been struggling internally, even though Denise and I continued to meet weekly. Though my professional life was showing great signs of success, I continued to have a heavy feeling in my chest. I felt sadness and disappointment.

My grandmother's health was declining, and I knew it was just a matter of time before she would make her transition. As I look back, I am grateful for my aunt and the rest of my family who helped my grandmother live with comfort and dignity until her final day. We should all be so lucky to live so comfortably and respectfully as we wind down our lives.

I had been home from work for about two weeks recovering from arthroscopic shoulder surgery when I found myself surfing the Internet for spine physical therapy jobs in California. The number of openings amazed me. Ever since I was a little girl, Hollywood had been on my radar. As fate would have it, I found an opening for a spine physical therapy job in Beverly Hills; as soon as I put it together, my resume was on its way.

I interviewed by phone for jobs in California and Arizona before I boarded a plane and headed to Rodeo Drive in Beverly Hills. I knew in my heart that my days in Kansas City would soon come to a close. The clinic in Beverly Hills was small compared to the clinic in Kansas City, and I could feel that I wasn't in Kansas anymore.

The night before the interview, I stayed in a five-star hotel on Rodeo Drive. I looked out my bedroom window at all the glitzy stores below. Many of the stores were closed, and the streets were bare, yet I was amazed by my presence there. I could feel the history of the setting. A week earlier, I had been talking with a friend about my desire to go to Hollywood, and suddenly I was there.

The interview with the physical therapy staff went well. However, I could feel that I was not a clinical match for what they were looking for. That night, as I boarded the plane for Phoenix, I wondered why my journey had led me to Hollywood at this point in my life if I wasn't a match. I wondered if my life's path would ever lead me back there.

Chapter 11
The Circle of Life

I Feel the Ease of Life
When Watching Birds Soar

How lucky am I to have a space that is all my own, where privacy with nature is greatly known. How lucky am I to have a place that I call my home, where the dreams of my heart are finally known. Treasured balcony, beautiful home, within your space I have transformed.

When you laid your foundation and built your walls, did you know your answer to my call? When you allowed me to find peace on your balcony for hours at a time, did you know of the wisdom that would become mine? And when the monsoons would come, and the rains would fall, did you ever know the peace of your metal roof wall.

Treasured balcony, beautiful home, did you know the ease of life that I would find when watching birds soar above this time? Perhaps one day, maybe soon, I will fly away from your loving cocoon. One last thought before I go—may the wisdom that has become my own somehow remain in the heart of this home.

I was to be interviewed for a physical therapy position in Globe, Arizona. I had scheduled the interview prior to leaving Kansas City, but my only real desire was to relocate to California and work in Beverly Hills. When I realized the job in Beverly Hills was not for me, I was grateful I had arranged job interviews in Arizona. I was excited for the opportunity that awaited me. I stayed the night in Phoenix because my flight from Los Angeles was late.

As I made my way from Phoenix to the small town of Globe that next morning, the beauty of the desert and the mountains mesmerized me. During the hour-and-a-half-drive into the high country, some of the most beautiful mountain ranges in the state of Arizona created a magnificent scenic byway on Highway 60.

Never before had I seen the sky so blue or a landscape so vast. I had never been in Arizona, but I was investigating the possibility of relocating to the desert. Since childhood, my spirit has always lived in the West. I could see what I had been feeling for years.

As I drove into the Globe-Miami area, as known by the locals, the evidence of a once-thriving economy and community could be seen in all of the vacant shops that lined the streets. The area was a time warp in some regards, but it was also what made it unique. Globe is situated in a valley and is surrounded by the Pinal Mountains. Copper mining has been at the heart of its economic foundation since before the turn of the nineteenth century.

The culture is largely Mexican-American, and the town boasts some of the greatest family-owned Mexican restaurants in Arizona. Many of the area's antique shop owners, artists, and healthcare professionals are transplants who have brought an array of cultural influences to the area. The San Carlos Apache Indian Reservation is thirty miles south of town.

When I arrived for my interview at the community hospital, I began to feel the unique opportunity before me. It was quite a contrast from where I had come from personally and professionally. Over the course of several hours, I met with the hospital administrative team and the physical therapy staff. I couldn't help but notice the sense of family that was prevalent among the hospital employees, and there was a genuine sense of caring. The fabric of the community was very different than anything I had ever known. I was starting to sense the quality of life for people in a smaller community. Many people find the pace of life attractive.

As my day unfolded, I seriously pondered the possibility of starting my life anew here. The tipping point in my decision to accept the job offer and move to Globe was meeting a middle-aged gentleman who was a local landlord. One of my biggest concerns was where would I find safe, comfortable housing. As fate would have it, he showed me a home that touched my heart, communicated that I would be safe, and told me the new life I was looking for awaited me in Globe, Arizona.

It was quite a change to consider moving from a city with over one million people to living and working in a town no bigger than eight thousand. And after the interview in Beverly Hills, the contrast couldn't have been more striking.

By the end of the day, I knew in my heart that I was going to accept the physical therapy position at the hospital and move my life to the Southwest. I was nervous about resigning my current physical therapy position in Kansas City and leaving my family and Denise. At the same time, I was excited about what was ahead of me.

On January 31, 2004, a close friend and I began the long trek to Globe. It was the dead of winter in the Midwest. The actual air temperature in Kansas City was zero degrees when we headed out. I was excited for the warmer temperatures that awaited me in Arizona, or so I thought. We arrived in Globe approximately a day and a half later, exhausted from the long car ride and from the stress of navigating mountainous terrain during a driving snowstorm.

I quickly learned that Old Man Winter really does exist in the desert. We were tired, but the reality of finally arriving was exhilarating. As I settled into my new home, there are no words to describe the gratitude I felt for the transition that was underway in my life. I could feel the magnitude of the new opportunity before me, and I knew my decision was my life's greatest choice to date.

On Monday, February 9, 2004, I began my employment at Cobre Valley Regional Medical Center. For the next eight years, the opportunity to raise my level of existence to world-class excellence was my passion.

Perhaps the greatest gift to come from my passion and from my move to the West was the day I realized that drugs were truly, finally a part of my past.

Just two months into my new life, I was presented with an opportunity to smoke marijuana. I had befriended a local guy, and he invited me to join him at a local club for karaoke. Later that evening, while attending an after-party, I was offered some pot. Long before I had moved West, I decided taking drugs was something that was not going to serve me well moving forward in my life, but the impulse to get high was still strong. I needed to get high one more time, it seemed.

When I did get high, something was very different. For the first time in my life, I missed being straight. Never before had I felt that way. Finally, the time had come when the quality of my life was better than the quality of being high. I had arrived at the rest of my life.

It has been many years since I last smoked marijuana, and my life has never been better. While I am fully aware that there are many people who choose to smoke marijuana and live productive, successful lives, it was not possible for me. As I look back, I understand that the universe provided the opportunity to know that that type of lifestyle did not fit the person I wished to become. I learned I didn't need it anymore.

When I moved West, I was given the opportunity to see a new world, physically, which helped me emotionally. The comfort and relief I had sought in drugs I now found in the landscape of the desert. What a healing environment I had been given. The presence of nature soothed my inner world and spoke volumes to my soul. I had come home to heal. Through exercise, my work as a physical therapist, and my relationship with Denise, I had discovered a powerful combination to live a successful, healthy life.

I think of people who have walked a similar path and who continue to do so for reasons that I know are right because only they know the perfection of their journeys. I have learned not to judge others. I learned this so powerfully from Denise; she always supported me unconditionally in all aspects of my life, even when my decisions may not have been her decisions for me. She trusted the process.

Today I have a healthy perspective. I trust that my life's path has excellence. Time spent in thought about my years taking drugs does not serve me. What serves me is my focus on what went right and what I have learned. Perhaps more than most, I appreciate a healthy body and mental clarity, something that drugs could have easily taken away. When I see others abusing mind-altering substances, I know that they are only trying to find their way, and I wish them well.

With the support of the hospital administration, I furthered my clinical expertise and became the director of physical therapy services. I know that none of this would have been possible if it hadn't been for the person who hired me, the physical therapy director at the time.

Through working with him and the totality of my time living and working in Globe, I learned that patients want to receive medical care from an organization that promotes love, respect, and world-class care. I learned patients want to come to a clinic that shows respect for their culture and for the community. I also learned that in allowing the goodness of the community to flow through the clinic, the healing energy of love becomes the foundation for a thriving clinic. Finally, and most of all, I learned the power of trust from the patient's perspective and the perspective of the hospital administration. When trust is present and never taken advantage of, living world-class excellence is then a possibility.

In order to make a difference in the lives of others, I must first make a difference in my own life. I know I can write from a perspective of knowing. I am a living example of what is possible in anyone's life with a strong desire and a lot of believing.

When I got high the last time, I created the opportunity to hear my heart's song for the first time. I knew that my desire to live world-class excellence in every phase of my life was real. I want to be an example for others to see that excellence is possible if we choose to focus our lives in that direction. When I realized that living life straight was better than living life intoxicated, I received the freedom to become my best.

When I think of how my life changed when I moved to Globe-Miami, Arizona, I am at a loss for words to describe the appreciation that I feel for the hospital and the people of this town. My only intention when I moved to this area was to be able to make a difference in the lives of the patients I treated. I was not expecting the magnitude in which the people of this area would make a difference in my life and how they would allow me to become the person I am today, both clinically and personally.

The people of Globe-Miami have shown me that the healthy, powerful love of family is the foundation from which all dreams can thrive. They have shown me that if you have good intentions to make a difference in the lives of others, the favor will be returned more than you can ever imagine. While this is not the reason to help others, it serves as evidence of the 'circle of life'.

I have learned to value the opportunity as a physical therapist to teach my patients about the body's ability to heal while teaching them about the excellence in life itself. How we chose to live each day goes a long way toward deciding what type of lives we will live, physically, mentally, emotionally, and spiritually.

Chapter 12

Healthy Living from the Inside Out

In a Gentle Breeze, I Know the Tenderness of My Heart

Gentle breeze, you are abundant. So soothing is your presence, so delicate is your touch.

Since childhood, I have felt your kindness. Today, I know your gift.

When you stir, my mind quiets, and my body can relax. The pores of my being open, and in an instant, I feel the tenderness of my heart.

Gentle breeze, you take me to a place where I feel love and appreciation, where I feel hope, and where I feel that I belong.

Gentle breeze, you are always welcomed, you are always cherished.

I served as the physical therapy director at at the hospital for three and a half years. My professional growth was significant during this time. Prior to becoming clinic director, I received training in the McKenzie system or Mechanical Diagnosis and Therapy (MDT) and was now practicing as a mechanical physical therapist, specifically treating patients suffering from neck and back pain while concurrently serving as clinic director.

During this time, my clinical skills reached new heights. I became proficient in the mechanical skills in which I had been trained and served as a clinic resource for other therapists utilizing mechanical therapies. I also served as a resource for local physicians as they began to learn of my advanced training. I was becoming the go-to person at the clinic.

Looking back, I realize the day that I was accepted into the diploma program at the McKenzie Institute International, was the day that my professional life found world-class excellence. Initially, I learned of the McKenzie system in 2004 while attending a one-day seminar in Las Vegas. While there, I learned of Robin McKenzie, a physiotherapist from New Zealand, who by accident, during the late 1950s, discovered the power of mechanical correction when treating a patient with low back pain. Through Robin, the McKenzie system or Mechanical Diagnosis and Treatment, was founded. He established the McKenzie Institute International in Raumati Beach, New Zealand, to provide advanced, international training for (Diploma) students who had successfully completed entry-level training within their own country. Robin established many national branches throughout the world to provide entry-level training for therapists and doctors. The national branch for the United States is located in Syracuse, New York. Robin McKenzie is a pioneer in the medical industry. His teachings and influence continue today.

The faculty, who presented the one-day seminar in Las Vegas were a mixture of national and international educators, and inspired me to learn more about this method of treatment. Through them, I could already see and feel the level of expertise present in the McKenzie system. I knew that my patient's would benefit greatly from this method of treatment. The faculty taught with great passion and commanded a level of respect.

I remember one faculty member who stood out in particular. She was powerful! I noticed how she would sit and stand. Her posture was amazing, erect. It communicated confidence, physical strength, health, and passion for life and the topic at hand. Her knowledge of the material was impressive, talking to a room filled with doctors, chiropractors, and physical therapists and answering their questions with ease. I took notice!

After completing my initial training, I earned entry-level credentialing in MDT in July 2006. As I trained, I was exposed to world-class talent through the faculty who presented the classes. I completed a series of six courses and the examination in eighteen months. It was a rapid pace, and I could not learn fast enough. Never before had I witnessed such a consistent level of clinical expertise of each faculty member. They inspired me to attain the same level.

In July of 2008, I successfully completed the diploma program, and became one of more than three hundred worldwide medical practitioners to earn diplomat credentials in MDT. Professionally, I had set myself apart. I had become a specialist within the practice of physical therapy. I had gained new tools and was creating my future success.

Perhaps the biggest surprise to unfold during this time was the day I discovered the title for my book and realized that it was time to share my life's story. It all came together one Saturday afternoon while I was away in Austin, Texas, completing my 9-week clinical residency that was required for the diploma program. I had continued my therapy with Denise while I trained in Texas. Our relationship was critical at this time since it helped me maintain my life's stability. Weekly, Denise and I would talk by phone, usually on Saturdays. I knew how fortunate I was that Denise would offer her time to me on the weekend. I could feel how much she cared.

On that particular Saturday, after Denise and I had talked, I drove myself to the local bookstore and found my usual studying spot. I was preparing for my upcoming exams that were required to complete the diploma program. Studying for hours at the bookstore, on weekends, brought me great comfort; it was one of my favorite times during the residency. I loved the opportunity to sit quietly and expand my mind. I was feeling incredibly grateful for Denise that day. I cannot remember the details of our conversation that morning, but I knew that my heart was on fire with appreciation for her support and love. I knew I had received greatly, enormously, the day I found her back in 1989.

As I tried to study, my attention was repeatedly pulled to what I was feeling and thinking … utter appreciation for Denise and her influence on my life. For so many years, she had stood by my side, helping me move past what troubled me and into a life that reflected the person who lived within me. I knew that the gift that I had received in Denise and our relationship was my life's greatest gift. She was my life's *primary gift*. As these words flowed into my mind, I wrote them down on a napkin. As I looked at the words, written in ink, I could feel their power and the accuracy that described her gift. I knew that the universe had spoken. I could feel the guidance that allowed this title to come forward. I realized that I was going to write a book and share my gift with the world.

It wasn't until the spring of 2012, following a full year of diligently writing much of my book, that the subtitle came forward, *Awaken to the Excellence of your Life's Journey*. This title was a perfect way to describe the contents of my book, my life, and the messages of inspiration and excellence that I wanted to share with the world. Again, I felt universally guided.

When I left the bookstore that day, I knew that my life had changed. I had discovered my life's primary gift—my relationship with Denise. Through her, I learned the perfection of my life's journey. She was the glue that held it all together. She was the reason I had come to see the excellence in my mother's schizophrenia, and she was the reason I was able to hear the call to light up the world. On that day, I could clearly see a bigger picture for my life and where I was headed once I completed my current studies.

My life had come together beautifully, although my success was not easy. My training and credentialing in the McKenzie system was by far the toughest experience I had encountered professionally. The required coursework, clinical training, and written and oral exams, pushed me to my academic limits. It was grueling. My desire to succeed and learn high-level skills allowed me to successfully reach the finish line. Clinically, it gave me the knowledge and skills I needed. I gained much confidence. As a therapist, I had found a higher level.

What I learned through the McKenzie system and the diploma program went far beyond the mechanical principles of therapy, clinical knowledge, expertise, or skill. Academically, I studied with people from around the world, and was educated by faculty from New Zealand, Australia, and the United States. I experienced how world regions and cultural differences impact learning styles, socialization, and standards of education, research, and faculty expectations. The academic standard was high. It was exciting to be part of an institution that promoted such learning. I was honored to take part in a program that united the world in positive outcomes for healthcare.

Already, I could feel my success. My advanced training through McKenzie International allowed me to expand my game, my life's experiences, and my mind, intellectually and creatively. I expanded my professional circle and discovered new employment possibilities and opportunities. Professionally and personally, I was able to identify my strengths and weaknesses against those of the world. I had come to know world-class excellence in a new way.

I have gained respect for those who have walked this journey. To become world-class excellence is a standard all its own. It is a focus of magnitude and intensity that creates empowerment, expertise, and endurance. To be world-class excellence is to be an athlete in life. As I succeed against competition in the world, I learn how to stand in a feeling place of belonging. I have gained respect for the credentials I have earned and the responsibilities to live those standards.

In healthcare and in all professions, I fully understand the public's desire to seek out professionals who have worked further to specialize and certify. It communicates a level of devotion and power that can be given to the patient through treatment, communication, and education. It communicates a commitment to excellence. Patients want to be in the hands of medical practitioners who have gone the extra mile. The patient knows intrinsically that they stand a better chance of going the extra mile in their own lives for healthcare, recovery, and wellness.

Following my training, I began to feel that I was making a significant difference as a clinical specialist. My patients were showing strong signs of healing, functional recovery, and positive outcomes. In my mind and to my own professional standards, I had become a true physical therapist. When I was in physical therapy school, I admired the level of expertise of the physical therapy faculty there. It was then that I first set into motion my desire to achieve a higher level of clinical expertise. Professionally, the faculty at Rockhurst University raised the bar for me and ignited the flame of clinical excellence within me. I carried it to the next level with mechanical therapy.

Mostly though, I realized that I had become a teacher. I had become a clinician with a great passion for teaching my patients about their bodies, the disease process, and recovery. As a teacher, I empowered my patients—through my passion—to take active roles in their healthcare. My patients quickly learned that passive, palliative care was not a practice that I routinely endorsed since it typically leads to poor long-term therapy outcomes. I looked to educate each patient about the importance of routine self-correction to help maintain therapy gains and reduce pain. I educated them about the importance of home compliance with therapy exercises to ensure successful long-term therapy outcomes, something I had learned emphatically from studying the mechanical principles of the McKenzie system.

As a teacher, I began to understand the powerful role I had been given as a healthcare professional. I began to understand just how fortunate, trustworthy, and responsible I was asked to be while standing so powerfully and guiding the lives of my patients.

As a clinic administrator, my lessons were just as powerful. Never before had I served as a director. Never before had I stood at the top of the professional chain, delegating responsibilities to others. To say that I was new to this is an understatement. I had never reached these heights as a clinician until I earned diplomat credentials in mechanical diagnosis and therapy. I had gained much confidence and was ready to serve as therapy director.

Early on, many of my administrative duties were tied to hiring a staff of physical therapists and replacing the department secretary who had just resigned. There was only one other therapist working in the clinic when I became director, a staffing problem that is all too real for physical therapy clinics in rural communities. I felt encouraged that the hospital administrators were confident in my leadership and decision-making skills as I moved forward to secure the future of the physical therapy clinic. I began to hire my staff.

As it turned out, through a professional acquaintance, I was introduced to a physical therapist in a private practice in Phoenix who was looking for per diem work as a means of supplementing his income. During our initial visit, I felt quite comfortable with him and respected what he had accomplished professionally. I felt incredibly appreciative that the universe had delivered a healthcare professional who was willing to work with a first-time director. He had more than thirty years of experience under his belt. I could feel the support of the universe guiding my life.

In the end, our professional relationship was a critical component of my overall success as therapy director. I learned much from him as he willingly shared his professional knowledge regarding departmental staffing, expenses, and handling patient concerns. I learned how to let the clinic run itself, avoiding micromanagement and staff negativity. I promoted an environment of professional autonomy and trust. It was a management skill that I had observed and appreciated in the previous physical therapy director.

Over the course of the next three plus years, I was successful in building a staff of six therapists and three secretaries. They were able to serve both the outpatient and inpatient physical therapy needs of Cobre Valley Regional Medical Center as well as providing weekend services that were previously unavailable. We had come a long way in a short amount of time from the number of employees on staff to the number of patients that we were able to treat in a day's time. And financially, we were making a significant difference for the hospital.

As director, I always made it a top priority to give frequent praise for a job well done. Over time, as we came together as a team, the power of our cohesiveness and the benefit of having diversified talent among the staff allowed us to provide quality healthcare that continues today.

Again, I am appreciative to the hospital administration and their unrelenting support of me and the rest of the therapy staff. The patients of the community and region were able to receive quality physical therapy services that are consistent with services provided in large cities. Too often, it is believed that small-town folks receive small-town care. As clinic director, I always emphasized to the employees I would hire not to let the size of an environment or town, dictate the person or the professional that you are. Rather, offer your character, passion, and desire to be the best to your patients and the world regardless of what surrounds you.

Perhaps one of my greatest thrills while serving as physical therapy director came during the early spring of 2010. The public relations department at the hospital asked me to do a one-time radio show for a local station. The idea was to discuss matters relating to mechanical physical therapy. It was an opportunity to showcase my skills as a specialized physical therapist and to further educate the community about the physical therapy services that were available to them.

Over time, it became clear to me—and others—that my passion for radio was real. "Healthy Living from the Inside Out," a monthly radio show, was born. Little did I know when I agreed to do my first show how much I would enjoy talking on the radio, although I was quite aware of my passion for teaching my patients. When the opportunity arrived to co-host my own local radio show to teach the community about healthcare, I was all in.

My greatest desire and thrill doing a monthly radio show was continuing to help make a difference in the community in which I lived and worked. As a physical therapist and healthcare provider, helping to make a difference in the lives of others is what I do! I am a professional that cares deeply. Radio was another avenue that allowed the passions of my heart to find their purpose and to be of service. It also meant a lot to me to further promote, through the radio program, the quality services offered by Cobre Valley Regional Medical Center.

Through radio, I grew tremendously. I gained respect for people who are able to think on their feet and communicate with clarity. I learned the power of preparation and rehearsal in bringing your best performance forward. I also learned the value of having fun while working and how to create an atmosphere of fun and frolic that creates success where all involved may benefit. Just as an athlete must feel his or her best physically, mentally, and emotionally to reach peak performance and help their team to win, we must do the same. For it is in the good feeling and higher vibration state of mind that all successful and deliberate creation begins, just as Abraham and Jerry and Esther Hicks remind us consistently through their teachings.

When I felt confident, inspired, and passionate from within, I took full responsibility for bringing my A game to the radio show. It was natural and evident in my voice, its tone, and through my energy and words to the audience. When I felt good, I was able to speak clearly, lovingly, and without hesitation. My thinking was quick and sharp. I stood with confidence and without judgment. Through radio—and life in general—I found that living and working in a playful atmosphere is one of the greatest tools for creating success in life.

On the radio, where voice matters most, I found that communication is where success begins. I also recognized that communicating from a place of knowledge and expertise is paramount, especially when speaking on matters related to healthcare. However, communicating from the heart is what builds trust and long-lasting relationships. To be genuine to others and yourself is the key for success.

For much of my adult life, finding my voice had been a tremendous challenge. I was so fearful and critical. Today, I more consistently speak lovingly to others and myself. Socially, I have struggled too, although most who know me would say differently. My struggles have been internal. Through radio, I came to appreciate the power of my voice. Today, I speak from the passions of my heart, confidently and with great energy. I feel less anxiety, personally, professionally, and socially. Finding my voice in radio gave my life new meaning. I stand empowered. I also found kindness and generosity.

Each month, as we prepared our show, I was appreciative of the healthcare providers of Cobre Valley Regional Medical Center and the other local and state healthcare organizations who came forward to share their passions and expertise. It helped our broadcast succeed. And, they did this without receiving any financial rewards. I know that I am not alone in the appreciation that I felt for the effort that was put forth by many of the healthcare providers, locally, nationally, and internationally, to educate the patients of our communities. So much of the time, I have found it is the generosity of others that allows us to know the goodness that lives within each of us.

During the fall of 2011, the pull to resign as physical therapy director was strong. From my life's teachers and life experiences, I intrinsically learned to listen for guidance from within. I could feel the call for something new. For some time, I had been feeling as though I had completed my journey as therapy director, yet I struggled with the idea of leaving the hospital and the physical therapy department. It was not easy to step away from something I had worked so hard to create. It had been my life's focus in one way or another for eight years. Working at the hospital and doing my radio program was my connection to the community. I didn't feel complete or ready to leave town, but I knew that my days as therapy director were coming to a close. It was time. I had completed my mission of helping to build a staff and clinic that could meet the physical therapy needs of the community. I could feel in my heart that my departure from the therapy department would not compromise the stability of the clinic.

On January 27, 2012, I resigned as director of physical therapy services at Cobre Valley Regional Medical Center. As it turned out, the CEO of the hospital, knowing that I had no immediate plans for moving out of the area, generously agreed to allow me to continue with my monthly radio show and to continue to represent the hospital through that medium.

About a month before I resigned, a professional acquaintance at another local healthcare company came to see me at the physical therapy clinic. I was surprised by her visit and knew that it must have been pretty important since she waited to speak with me for nearly thirty minutes. I was behind in patient care and could not break away. When we talked, she spoke of a physical therapy position that had just recently opened. It was an opportunity to provide home physical therapy services locally. She was in search of a physical therapist to fill this need. As I listened to the details of the job, I felt that my next professional endeavor was upon me.

I knew the opportunity to direct and manage a physical therapy clinic successfully was critical for my overall growth. Today, I stand more confident and have greater clarity regarding the accomplishments of my life and my ability to be a leader. I appreciate the relationships that I formed with hospital leadership. I worked closely with other department directors and hospital administrators while attending leadership meetings, training, and retreats. I felt at home with them, cognitively, emotionally, and mentally. I enjoyed the high level of professionalism, respect, and support. Mostly, I appreciated the focus on results and finding reasons for our success instead of focusing on what was wrong or who was to blame. As therapy director, I found my place within the hospital organization and my place as a leader. I felt like an important member of a successful team. I felt respected and was encouraged to share my ideas. I felt inspired to be my best for the team. I had found a professional family that I came to love and considered home.

Financially, I changed. I found freedom. Today, I am able to choose a life that more truly reflects the desires of my heart rather than the basics of my life. Surprisingly, I have found respect for having less rather than having more. As director, my earning potential was greater. I was finally able to buy the things that I had always wanted. Initially, I allowed myself to play. I did not feel the stress of financial pressures, which was a new freedom. I bought a new car with comfortable, leather seats, something that I had always wanted. I traveled more and bought gifts for family and friends. Finally, I could express to others the generosity of my heart.

Interestingly though, from material abundance, I began to understand that the most prized possession is what money cannot buy. The gift of happiness comes from within, and I was feeling happier than at any other time in my life. I started to realize the true gift I had received. With time and understanding, I learned how to save money, perhaps the best gift of all. In doing so, the power of money became less of a force in my life as my financial savings accumulated. Few of my choices were reflective of monetary needs. Through savings, I provided myself the opportunity to be more selective in my professional choices.

I was able to make more choices of the heart, choices that reflected the passions of my life. I was able to look into my future and decide to step away as therapy director rather than hanging on to my job just for the paycheck. I realized that I was starting to create the life I had always wanted.

As I gained experience with having and saving larger amounts of money, through my life's choices, I was showing the universe that I was truly able to handle any amount of money that comes my way, now or in the future. I was showing the universe that the success I had gained during my clinical training and practice and service as clinical director was stable within me.

I also began to understand the concept of the next logical step that Abraham and Jerry and Esther Hicks refer to so often in their teachings. From them, I've come to know and witness how life provides a ladder to climb comfortably to accomplish our greatest dreams. It allows us the opportunity to ascend in vibration, to feel good more and more of the time as we take these incremental steps. We ascend in manifestations, in life's responsibilities, sequentially, so that we grow and evolve at a comfortable pace and allow our dreams to ease into our lives. Logically and at the right time, we take steps so life does not knock us over with all we have asked for. It is the kindness of the universe influencing our lives in the gentlest ways. It is learning the art of allowing.

From my earliest years, I asked for much greatness in my life. I struggled for years. From childhood to my early adult years, I could not gain positive momentum in my life. As I began to work with Denise and my other life's teachers, matters began to fall into place, one by one and year after year. My life was unfolding with unquestionable precision, guiding me toward my dreams. I was able to handle more responsibility while feeling better and better each day. Until one day, when I didn't feel well, I recognized that it was time to make a change and take the next logical step.

Chapter 13

Nature, a Portal for Knowledge

Beautiful Tree

Beautiful tree, I honor you. So radiant are your offerings. So brilliant is your quiet presence—never intrusive with your knowing. You embody the truth of a great teacher, for those who can hear and for those who will listen. In you, I have found a great role model. From you, I learn how to allow.

When the storms come and deliver great force against you, so magnificent is your flexibility, so intrinsic is your allowing. And when the storms pass and you drink the nutrients left behind, so precisely, I can understand that the storms of my life are the nutrients for my soul. And as I watch you grow, and your stability reaches far beneath into mother earth, the height of your existence can now be understood.

Beautiful tree, from you I learn that if I am to grow tall and mighty in my character and if I am to offer love from my being, the foundation from which I stand must be mighty and loving. From you, I learn that if I am to serve as a loving extension from mother earth, in which all living creatures can find shelter, then, I must do so equally and, without judgment.

From you, I learn that if I am to be a great teacher, then I must stand quietly with my knowing and trust that those who seek my wisdom will hear me when they are ready. Beautiful tree, with clarity, I know your wisdom and feel your love. You are the connection between the earth and sky. You are a portal for knowledge.

took a month off after leaving the hospital, which provided the opportunity to refocus my energy and my life in a new direction. I was exhausted from the last month of work at the hospital. There was much to attend to as I wrapped up my job. In March, 2012, I began my work as a home physical therapist. I had agreed to work full-time for a local company, providing home physical therapy services for the patients of the Globe-Miami area and other communities within an hour's drive. I spent several weeks in training to learn the specifics of homecare before I was able to treat patients on my own.

One early evening while driving home from Phoenix, I began to notice strong communication between the mountains of the high desert and myself. I was feeling especially good that day since I had just completed one and a half weeks of training for my new job and was eagerly heading home to reunite with Walter and Ethel, my two beautiful, loving Chihuahuas.

I had driven this terrain many times and always took notice of the power of the landscape. Yet, on this particular evening, as the sun was descending in the west and still in full view, I could feel and see the wisdom of these mountains as never before. I was euphoric; the energy of health hung so magnificently in the air. It was on full display, in the light of the sun and on the top and sides of the mountains. Like never before, I could see health as energy. I fully understood that health is the energy of love, rich love that is so massive in its presence and absent of resistance.

As I drove, I could read the energy so purely. I felt breathless and euphoric in its presence. I did not resist. Several days later, I wrote a letter to Denise, describing the elation I was feeling in more detail. I was floating. The portal between physical and non-physical was thinner than thin. I almost didn't see the road as my eyes wanted to constantly look at the vibration I was feeling and witnessing. I wanted to gaze and read this energy like never before. There was much vibrational knowledge there—it was godly. The miracle of healing occurs in this energy. This energy dissolves illness in all forms, period! This experience continues within me today.

I began my work as a home physical therapist and while still driving in the presence of these same mountains, my strong communication with non-physical energy continued. What a gift I was receiving. I began to sense the non-physical energies that currently called these mountains home. I began to feel the influence of their presence in the persons who physically lived on this land. I was uplifted beyond words.

As I drove to patients' homes, I had a great deal of time to share with these non-physical energies. I began to think of the vast knowledge that is available for all humans if we only choose to tune into the non-physical energy that is present all around and within the land. As I have learned so well from Abraham and Jerry and Esther Hicks, when our physical bodies are gone, our energies carry on in the non-physical realm. However, it remains focused on physical matters just as keenly as when we are embodied.

As I began to treat patients in their home, I couldn't help but notice how my energy was shifting and changing so dramatically from the energy that I carried when I was working at the clinic. I was quickly transforming my vibration. On many days, I felt euphoric. My heart was exploding with love and appreciation for what was unfolding within me.

I couldn't help but notice the impact that my new level of energy had on my relationships with my patients. I found myself wanting to tell my patients how much I loved them. I had never felt such love for my patients—or felt such love from them in return. I had found a new level. Again, I was floating through my physical existence.

I looked forward to the drive each day and to my rich communication with non-physical energies. I had never seen the light of nature shine as brightly as when the landscape of the desert was in full view. Most days, while driving, I could see the treetops glisten in the sunlight, and I felt a new, sincere appreciation for the deep colors in nature. Often, I found myself breathing deeply. At times, the power of this environment left me breathless. I felt genuine appreciation for my journey.

My physical perceptions had changed; my energies were merging consistently with the landscape. I felt as though I was looking at nature deeply and communicating with precise clarity. In this energy, I felt knowledge. I could see that the loving radiance of nature was where the most powerful existence lives. In nature, there is incredible love, incredible power, and precision. There is no resistance.

To speak of the knowledge that lives within nature knows no limits. It is infinite intelligence, as Abraham and Jerry and Esther Hicks teach. In humans, this source of energy is present—however only to the degree it is recognized. In this energy, I felt harmony, ease of life, and tranquility. I felt my inner genius strongly. I knew that the wisdom that lives in nature was a gift for those who can hear it.

From a physical therapy perspective, my focus had changed. Quickly, I found myself mastering computer documentation and helping the patients restore functions while continuing to live at home. This was a far cry from treating patients in the clinic, mechanically, where the focus of therapy was specifically on joint integrity and quality of movement.

In homecare, the focus was on treating the whole patient. We assessed heart rates, blood pressure, and body temperatures. We educated patients about medication. We checked for bedsores and monitored cognitive changes and depression. Physical therapy was just a part of the services we provided. It was a whole new ballgame. I had so much to learn.

While my work environment changed considerably as I transitioned professionally, my confidence in patient care remained consistent. From my earliest years as a therapist, I always felt comfortable and confident in healthcare matters. My ability to intuitively know the patient has been my strongest professional attribute. Once I met a patient, it did not take me long to assess their needs and find restorative care.

As I became more comfortable with the workings and pacing of my new job, I was hitting my stride. I began to understand the true focus of physical therapy homecare—patient safety. I found myself truly enjoying helping the patient learn how to stay safe at home while standing, walking, and going outdoors. Mostly, I could feel the sincere appreciation that my patients held for someone who cares for their wellbeing. I enjoyed working with the patient in surroundings that allowed them to be most comfortable. It gave them a means to exercise independence while engaging in therapeutic, teaching relationships.

As people age, they lose the ability to negotiate space. They may lose peripheral vision while driving or the ability to determine physical proximity to objects in a room. Something as simple as sitting in a chair can become a hazard. As people lose space relations, falling becomes a great concern. Similarly, as people physically weaken, they may lose the ability to stand or walk without assistance. As a home physical therapist, much of my work was educating patients and family members on ways to promote home safety when performing the activities of daily living.

My work in physical therapy homecare has shown me the massive need for such services, locally, nationally, and perhaps internationally. I have a greater understanding of the role that home healthcare plays in allowing persons to stay in the home as they age. I have gained much admiration and appreciation for healthcare workers who provide such services for the many persons in need. The demand for this kind of care will only increase as the population ages. In a small community like Globe-Miami, where medical resources are limited, a patient's ability to stay safely in his or her home, where the love and the attention of family is strong, is essential for the patient's overall well-being and longevity. Healthcare organizations that provide home services are critical parts of our healthcare industry and will be for years to come.

While I felt genuine appreciation for the opportunity to provide home therapy and felt fully supported by my company, I quickly tired of the other job-related responsibilities. The hours required to document, drive to the patient's homes, and return phone calls and e-mails left me physically and emotionally depleted. For me, homecare became a seven-day-a-week job. I was exhausted.

For several months, I had been feeling the desire to walk away from therapy altogether, and for an unknown period of time. Something different was calling me. I could feel it daily. My feelings were so strong. My communication with the universe during my daily drives only helped clarify the dreams of my life. I could feel them closer than ever before. It was time to truly pay attention.

On one beautiful Sunday afternoon, I was working on material for my radio show on my balcony. I felt a little bird fly toward my head. I was startled. Never before had I been approached by nature in this way while sitting on my balcony. Thirty minutes later, I discovered the little bird resting on my kitchen floor.

She was a beautiful little baby bird, alert and healthy. She was sitting so quietly and peacefully. I was so surprised and delighted to find her. I sensed divine intervention and communication with the universe, yet I was unsure of the message. My mind began to focus on the bird's safety and returning this fragile little creature to nature. Before I knew it, she had scurried behind the refrigerator, completely out of sight and out of reach. I could feel her fear.

Cautiously, I took the handle of a long broomstick and gently tried to find her. As I did, I noticed a piece of paper wedged between the refrigerator and a cabinet. As I reached for it, I could see small words typed on the page. It was a poem written by Margaret Stortz.

Let's Begin Again
A Reflection to Begin the New Year

Here we are, at the doorway of a new year. It is for us to make of this gift what we will. With this idea in mind, let's look at a little story written by Minnie Louise Hoskins and used by King George VI in his 1939 Christmas broadcast to the English people.

"I said to the man who stood at the gate of the Year, 'Give me a light that I may tread safely into the unknown.' And he replied, 'Go out into the darkness and put your hand into the hand of God. That shall be to you better than light and safer than a known way!'"

Could we not think about this small admonition as this year begins to unfold? Yes, we have made plans, and perhaps we are completing other plans. Yet there is always the unknown that lies in wait as well. We can be wise and begin the year by turning regularly to God for guidance and light. The world is full of uncertainty, and many things are beyond our control. The believer can be sure of only one thing: your unity with God.

Perhaps it's more effective to go forth into the unknown, into the unlit corridors of the future with plans made, dreams unsheathed, lightly and flexibly so that we can make quick turns if needed. When we know that the light of God is always within us, we shall find that we are always in the right place.

As I read this beautiful poem, I felt the wisdom and accuracy of its content for my own life. I knew that I was being divinely led to release my fears and step into the unknown path before me. I was to hold the hand of God and the energy of the loving universe in my mind for guidance and safety. Through this poem, I gained courage, clarity, and focus. It was time to step into the life that I had worked so hard to create and to move forward with the knowledge that the universe was standing beside me, closer than ever.

I went back to my computer, but my thoughts remained with the beautiful little bird that had so eloquently touched my life. She remained hidden in my kitchen. My hope was to safely return her to the loving environment from where she had come. Intuitively, I knew she was frightened. I decided to let her rest and recover from the trauma of her ordeal.

For the next two hours, as I worked at my computer on the balcony, I did not hear a peep from her. I began to worry that she may never come out. I decided to take action. As I pulled my refrigerator forward, I saw her cuddled in a corner, frightened as could be. I knew that she was ready to be freed.

Gently, I placed her in an empty shoebox and covered her as I transported her outside. Dusk had fallen, and there was no sight of unwanted predators. I decided to place her under a nearby tree. As she sat in her box, I made sure that she would be able to free herself from her confines when she was ready.

As I walked away from her, I thanked her again for her gift in my life. I prayed to the universe for her safety as I released her back into nature. The next morning, I decided to return to the tree to check on her whereabouts. She was nowhere in sight. I trusted that the universe had delivered again.

For some time, I had been feeling uneasy about working strictly as a physical therapist. My internal life was evolving at a rapid pace, and my professional desires were reflective of these changes. Genuinely, I still enjoyed teaching my patients about medicine, their bodies, and recovery, but much more was calling me now. More and more, during patient care, I found myself wanting to talk with patients about the spirits that lived within them, the fuel for life that would lead them to their greatest knowing of happiness and health. I wanted to talk to my patients about healing from the inside out, through deliberate, positive thought and imagery while continuing to utilize the best that medicine and therapy offered. More and more, I wanted to share with my patients the energy that lived within me. It's the electric, positive force energy, and it has served me well in creating my best life, in health, wealth, and wisdom. It can also serve others.

For years, during meditation, I envisioned myself living the life of my dreams. I saw myself standing tall—confidently, lovingly—as I meet the heroes in my life. I would share my message of inspiration and excellence with my heroes by writing my book, speaking to audiences of all ages, and taking part in a show that lights up the world and leaves the audience inspired to live their best lives in spirit, passion, and wisdom.

I would create my own radio show and encourage my guests to speak of the passions of their hearts in all areas of their lives and the wisdom that has come from their journeys. I would envision owning my own physical therapy practice and creating an environment of love, passion, fun, and world-class care. I envisioned creating a foundation of excellence that provides avenues for others to live their dreams. And I would create a sanctuary in nature where the domestic animals of our planet would have the chance to live in luxury and comfort. I saw myself sitting peacefully, feeling free of life's pressures and living the generosity that has always been alive in my heart. During meditation, I gained strength and knowledge that this life of my dreams was mine to create. In my heart and my mind, I was already there. It was time to live my visions.

To make this happen, I resigned as a homecare physical therapist. My stay was short, but it somehow felt right. The message from the universe was consistent and guided me steadily. I struggled when saying good-bye to my patients, but they all wished me well. They understood how much I wanted to follow my dreams. I felt their support. During therapy, my patients and I often talked of matters of the heart. It provided an opportunity for patients to release some of the stresses of life and helped them heal. Our discussions would unfold naturally during the course of our time together. I realized that we were truly there for each other. We genuinely brought out the best in each other. Even so, my professional responsibility to my patients was always at the forefront.

Just a week after leaving homecare, I received a phone call from the owner of the company. He wanted to discuss a new opportunity that he had in mind that would allow us to continue to work together. I was surprised and delighted to hear from him. I wondered how often people walk away from a company and then are asked to return. I felt the presence of the universe, and I felt appreciated. We had a relationship of mutual respect and a passionate desire to help others in need.

He shared his idea of having me serve as the marketing representative for his company. When I initially joined him, the number of patients requiring homecare sharply increased. He believed my influence was the difference. At the same time, he was fully aware of my need to step away from patient care. He was aware of the tremendous drain I had been feeling during my last days at the hospital and while providing homecare with his company, but he wanted to continue to utilize my passion for therapy and my medical expertise in a way that would benefit those in need.

During the short time that we had worked together, he had come to understand the love relationship I had developed with the patients of my community through my work at the hospital, the radio show, and his company. He could feel the powerful ties that bonded me to the area. He also knew about the trusting professional relationships I had developed with the local medical community. He had a vision to expand upon that success.

It didn't take much convincing, and I agreed to rejoin him in early August, less than one month after I resigned from patient care. I was ecstatic to be back on board to further assist his efforts to provide home health services to the region. I appreciated the opportunity to continue helping the community that I had grown to love—and to do so in a way that would not leave me feeling exhausted or depleted. I appreciated the opportunity to make a difference in the lives of others.

I couldn't help but notice the perfection of the universe precisely displaying the next logical step in my life. With the help of a little bird one Sunday afternoon, I was guided to hold the hand of the universe and open a new door in my life. I felt the power of faith and the power of inner guidance. What a perfect fit, it seemed. It was an opportunity to use my voice again, to allow the passions of my heart to have a purpose, and to provide a much-needed service.

As I moved forward in this new way, I did so with certainty that when hearts of passion come together with an intention to help better the lives of others, and to bring world-class healthcare to the people of rural communities, successful outcomes will prevail. From positive focus comes a positive life.

In February 2013, I said goodbye to Globe-Miami, Arizona, and relocated my life to Sierra Vista, Arizona, where I currently reside as this book is being written. I have returned to working as a physical therapist in an outpatient therapy clinic and do so knowing that providing physical therapy services is a powerful way in which I can be of service to the world! My work as a marketing representative was short lived yet undeniably accurate during that time in my life. It provided an opportunity for me to realize that my work as a physical therapist was truly a significant aspect of my life's journey and a genuine part of who I am. And, it afforded me time to step away from patient care just long enough to rest, restore, and to realize just how much I enjoy helping others to heal.

When I relocated to Globe-Miami in February of 2004, my desire was to help the people of this community to live better lives. During my first visit, in November 2003, I could feel their needs—and I could feel their love. I wanted to be of service through my knowledge of medicine and physical therapy and the passions of my heart. Today, these desires continue within me.

While visiting with my family recently, I was asked how I had grown since moving to Arizona. I did not know where to begin. My growth had been tremendous. I shared how I learned to focus outwardly, radiating the loving source of the universe, while allowing the excellence of our world to live within me. I shared how I learned to trust the perfection of each person's journey, and how I found greatness and allowing there. More so, I had become a person of service, assisting others from a place of tremendous spirit in a way that allowed the spirit within me to stay true to myself. I was a different person. I had become the butterfly.

When I left the hospital and the physical therapy clinic, I knew about the transformation that had taken place within me. Yet, my time in home healthcare was still before me. My spiritual journey in the desert landscape had yet to unfold. My relationship with non-physical energy had yet to find its new place within me. In just a few months, I would expand again.

Through my work in homecare, I became closer to the heart of my community and to my own heart within. I felt the power of the human spirit stronger than ever. I discovered the spirit that was alive within the landscape of this area. I had learned that there is no more sacred place than being invited into the home of another. To see others as they live in their homes is to see the person that lives within them. One of the greatest gifts of the heart is treating others and their belongings with respect no matter what their living conditions and no matter how they treat their own belongings. It demonstrates the God within. It accesses the love of the universe.

I saw poverty and felt the exhaustion that comes with living in this energy. I stepped into patients' homes that had no air conditioning when outside temperatures were well above a hundred degrees and experienced a fraction of the hardship in which they lived. I witnessed the "grace of grandmothers" in homes where the elderly were cherished, nurtured, and provided for. I witnessed the hardship of living alone with a physical disability or being cared for by family members who were unable to cope. I saw how providing physical therapy in the home gives a deeply independent person the dignity and strength to find his or her way back to a quality life.

My world expanded. I saw much in a short amount of time. My time spent in homecare touched me deeply. From the richest to the poorest, I gained much respect for the people of Globe-Miami as they let me into their homes and into their lives. I had learned greatly through cultural diversity. Since I am so sensitive to energy, perhaps my lessons go beyond what most would encounter. I am a person of the heart, I cherish what I have learned, and I realize that these are their journeys. I respect the presence and trust the knowledge of the universe.

As a professional, I came to this community with knowledge and expertise. As a human being, I came with love, passion, and wisdom. As a professional, I found a desire for health, wellbeing, and education among the people. As a human being, I found humility, love of family, tradition, and acceptance. In spirit, I found the opportunity to be the person I came here to be.

Chapter 14

Awaken to the Excellence
of Your Life's Journey

At Daybreak,
I Feel the Opening of God's Hands

Breathe deeply and awaken. Feel the opening of God's hands as daybreak settles on the morning horizon, and the light of day arouses the earth. The gift of life is fresh in the air, and the sounds of nature have begun their calls.

Now open your eyes to the world that lives within your heart, and radiate the light of your shining star. The heart of God is within you now. The heart of the universe surrounds you now.

Breathe deeply and awaken. Trust the excellence of your life's journey and appreciation for all that is will find your heart. Believe in the power of your dreams; they will create your greatest life. Deliver your gifts to the world, and the world will give you life's greatest gifts.

From a place of self-love and respect, I have awakened to the excellence of my journey. Early in my life, I faced great challenges. I could not be a child like my siblings or my classmates. My journey was different. In my school, I learned about schizophrenia, struggling to breathe, and dealing with physical violence. My teacher was very powerful.

As an adolescent I began to use drugs. My father was never a part of my life, and my mother suddenly vanished one day while I was at school. I became a ward of the court and completed my high school education while living in a state group home. At twenty-six, I met an exemplary professional who began to show me the way, mostly through love. For twenty years and beyond, I learned lessons of discipline, love, and respect for self and others. I learned of my love for academics and physical fitness, and I eventually became a licensed physical therapist with a specialty in mechanical therapy. I also learned lessons of great humility when I was assigned the legal guardianship of my mother, and it was then that I became her friend.

In 1999, I became *on fire for my life* because of the excellence I had witnessed in another human being. I began to dream of talking to the world about the excellence that lives within each of us—but only when I could do so from my own place of excellence. Gradually, I freed myself from drug use and relocated to the Southwest. In the desert, I began to hear my heart's song and awaken to the excellence of my life's journey. I gained mental clarity and discovered the wisdom of my life's teachings. No matter where you start in life, no matter what your circumstances, a life that you can dream, you can live fully. The key is to permit your story to unfold in a way that allows you to move past what inspired you to make a change, and then to become that change.

From the universe and from loving, qualified professionals, I asked for assistance to become this change. I continuously looked for the answers that allowed my success through education, physical fitness, psychotherapy, spiritual teachings, and helping others. I began to utilize the love of my heart and the creativity of my mind rather than the troubles of my mind to lead me each day. I discovered the power of positive thought and unrelenting focus on my life's dreams. I utilized the resources of our world and eventually opened the door to what was possible in my life. I allowed the greatness in others to teach me about the greatness that lived within me. For it is known, that which we admire in others is merely a reflection of what lives within us.

I have learned how to clear the debris from my path by being ruthless in my life's choices, professionally and personally. In doing so, I am able to make more powerful decisions and associate myself with those who have my best interests at heart and share a common bond of electricity, passion, and excellence for life. I have allowed appreciation to find my heart—for all that I have seen, for all that I have lived, and for all the people I have known. I am learning to cherish all that is life, and I am learning to cherish the teacher I have become.

Allow the light to shine on all that is good, and recognize the champion that lives within you. The success of your life begins with the success of your relationship with you. How you treat yourself is truly how you will treat others and the world. Be kind, gentle, rewarding, and generous to yourself every day. Focus your mind on your dreams, and your dreams will become a reality.

Find love, respect, and forgiveness for yourself, and you will then forgive, respect, and love others. For it is from the enormous power of a loving, stable relationship that all abundant life can evolve. Ask yourself who you want to be in this world. No one can truly see what lives within your heart. People will see what you show them, and most will not look beyond that. Allow your creative mind and inner genius to emerge and become part of the world where only excellence lives.

As I awaken to the excellence of all that I have lived, I have come to realize it is okay to have a journey that is not typical and to emerge on the other side, standing tall. We all have unique individual life stories. This is life's primary gift!

I have learned that when one person in a family benefits from psychotherapy, many benefit. I have learned how to hear the person behind schizophrenia and how to have the courage to be there when needed. I have learned that by standing in a place of inspiration, even persons with mental illness can be called to a place that is greater than what limits them. I have learned that mental illness is only the vehicle in which our lessons are carried.

Had I not had my mom as a teacher, and the great teacher Denise, none of this would have been possible. The contrast between my mom and her illness and loving, professional, Denise, is a union that only the universe could have orchestrated. It was a perfect fit for me. It gave me what I needed.

The universe sent me several powerful teachers, and the lessons learned with each have been profound. From my mother, I learned to look beneath the surface of her schizophrenia to find her genius and her royalty that lived so deeply within her. I also learned humility and inner strength beyond description, which helped my character evolve. From Denise, I learned the excellence of respect for self and others and the enormous power of a loving, stable relationship/foundation from which all abundant life can evolve. From Denise, I received my life's primary gift and awakened to the excellence of my life's journey! From Celine, I discovered world-class excellence and began to dream of what was possible for my life. From Celine, I received the energy to create my best life.

Ultimately, I learned how to show up for myself through my choices, which allowed me to show up for others. Denise taught me this when she showed up at eight o'clock for a session when half of the city was dark due to a power outage. That morning, we had had an ice storm in Kansas City, and the building in which Denise practices had no electricity. Denise was the only one who showed up in her building, and she left a canteen light right outside her door to light the way for me!

I have learned how to love from a place of health. I have learned how to respect others, the process of life, and myself. I have learned that great teachers come in many forms. I do not judge my teachers; I hold them in the highest regard because I wouldn't be the person I am today without their teachings.

I want my life's journey to demonstrate what is possible when a person seeks the opportunity in life's adversity. Let your direction in life and your internal happiness be your measuring stick for where you stand instead of letting your shortcomings lead your life. While I know that

I have fallen short in many phases of life, my desire is to become world-class excellence, live world-class excellence, and admire the world-class excellence in others.

Be on fire for your life everyday, and watch the incredible life that unfolds before you!

Chapter 15

Hand in Hand

Trust, When Present,
Is the Safest Place in the Universe

At eight years old, I lost my way. Suddenly and traumatically, those who surrounded me could no longer reach me. The hysteria of mental illness had taken its toll. On this night, our mother was taken from our home.

I was frightened for what was to come, for my mom, for myself, and for my family. No longer could I feel the trusting presence of the universe and the safest place that I had ever known. No longer could I trust the word of another. On that night, I became my own parent and a child of the universe looking for guidance.

Now, I have returned to the safest place that I have ever known. Through the loving heart of another, I have returned to the loving guidance of my inner universe. With love, I have learned that when you can trust the word of another, safety has been provided. I have learned that when you are able to keep your word to yourself, there is no safer place.

*D*uring my sessions with Denise, I would sometimes say, "Godmother, you are God's answer for nature's imperfections." "How beautiful," Denise would reply.

During our years of working together, Denise and I shared hours of love, deep trust, and perseverance. I started to believe and witness how nature can magnificently balance itself in the most unusual ways with incredible precision. I started to believe and witness that my life was somehow detailing for me, through contrast, the perfection of the universe in a glorious way.

What I had lost in my relationship with my mother, I was able to receive from the loving relationship I had with Denise. What I had found in the relationship with my mother, the teachings of her schizophrenia, I could never have found if my mother had been of a healthy mind. Through the universe and the balancing of nature, the excellence of my life's journey was unfolding. I was unwrapping my life's primary gift.

As I have learned through the teachings of Abraham and Esther and Jerry Hicks, words do not teach. Instead, our feelings and our experiences are our greatest teachers. It is my desire to share one of the most powerful letters that I have ever written to Denise during our more than twenty years of working together.

Through my letter, it was my intention to provide Denise, a clear picture, an experience, of the totality of my relationship with my parents, the appreciation they have for the professional woman who stepped into my life, and the accuracy in which the universe seeks balance and goodness. May the teachings of my journey find their highest purpose and serve you.

Any parent could have written this letter to the person who comes forward and provides incredible acts of love and guidance for a child. Because my mother has schizophrenia and my father was absent, a letter physically written by them to Denise was not possible. With time, I began to feel a strong appreciation from my parents toward Denise for her role in my life. And I felt the urge to write Denise on behalf of them in 2008 and subsequently shared it with her.

Hello, Denise. I am Kelly's father, and her mother stands here beside me. We are the biological parents of Kelly and her three siblings. We are here to thank you for all you have done for our daughter.

We have disappointed Kelly as parents. Our struggles did not allow her and her siblings the opportunity to observe and learn from healthy parental role models. We come to you today as aged parents. We are able to see how you have provided Kelly with the strength and love of two parents. Now as an adult, she stands strong and proud in front of us.

She tells us this is the first conversation that she has ever had with her parents together. She tells us that her childhood broke her spirit and her character. She says she has been broken for most of her life and has operated in the world as many of her internal parts separated at birth. We had no idea what happened to our daughter. She tells us that this has made her want to kill herself since she was eight years old. She also says we will never know all the sadness that has been trapped inside of her. She tells us this sadness is the part of Kelly that we do not have a right to know. The only Kelly she will bring to us today is the one who stands in front of us who has godly love for all humans. She tells us you have earned the right to know her sadness, and you have done our work for us.

With Kelly's permission and assistance, we would like to offer our apology to you for the enormous void we left in the life of Kelly and her three siblings. You have done the work of two parents, and you have helped us more than words can say. In a way, we had given Kelly up for adoption to the universe. She knew something was not right with us.

She comes to us today, asking for our forgiveness. She wants to be considered your daughter. She tells us that in the years she has known you, you have not once turned your back on her.

Hello Denise, I am Kelly's mother. Kelly is my angel. I don't know why I'm so attached to her, but it happened the day she was born. She came into this world with the determination to not be abused. She asked God to put a shield around her to protect her physically from harm and to give her the wisdom to know how to communicate with me. I developed rheumatic fever when I was a young child. I believe it caused some type of damage to my brain that eventually led to my schizophrenia. Kelly has felt trapped between her siblings and me since she was two years old. She understood that she must show me love in order to remain safe. Her sister, my eldest daughter, frustrated me, so I hit her. I was unable to stop myself. My two sons really needed their father. My eldest son had a few brief encounters with his father and witnessed the heartache between the two of us. After that, he never wanted to be around his father again. My sons became strangers to me while they were little boys. My parents stepped in to help with my children's care, but I made sure that my parents did not take my children away from me.

I actually lost all four of my children when they were very young. I was mentally and physically ill. Kelly became out of control. She was afraid of me, was sad for me, and hated me. My children have lived with a lot of violence, sadness, chaos, and fear due to my illness and the absence of their father. Every day, I live with not knowing my children. My illness has prevented me from being a mother.

I know that Kelly needed a true mother—a mother who she could love with all of her heart, safely. I know all of my children have needed a mother who could provide for them, as I have been unable to do. As I have grown older, my children stay away, except for Kelly. About ten years ago, I was hearing voices to cut an artery. Kelly found it necessary to provide me with a chance to live. I can never understand why she would do this when I have never been a mother in the way she needed. I believe she taught herself how to be an adult by being my parent.

In reality, Kelly has become my parent, I have seen her treat me the way she always wanted me to treat her. She has taught me about respecting other people, their time, and their desires. She taught me about boundaries, organization, health and fitness, and about God.

I know that I cannot take credit for the Kelly I see today. I know that much of the credit must go to you for the love you have given my *daughter. I know when she says your name Denise there is a glow to her that tells me everything.*

You have helped my daughter and me and the rest of our family in a way that has reshaped our experience of life. I wish I could have been a wonderful mother for my children. In my heart, I love my children just as any mother loves her children. In my mind, my illness separates me from my children, my family, and a normal life. Although I cannot come to you physically and thank you for being there for Kelly, I can thank you in this letter for being the strong mother she so critically needed. I can only communicate my gratitude and appreciation to you through her heart.

As I read this letter to Denise, I felt as though she finally understood the totality of her presence in my life, within my family and the magnitude of thankfulness that lives within my heart for her. For years, I would tell Denise just how much I treasured her in my life, our work together, and the love and respect she helped me create for myself. My appreciation for her could not live quietly within me. It beats strongly.

Somehow, my words of appreciation to Denise always left me feeling empty in my heart. It was as though, in my mind, I knew that Denise could not fully see her gift to my family and me. Today, my heart knows differently. As I shared this letter with Denise, I could sense her level of understanding, deepening. The presence of my parents was real and communicated a level of appreciation for her that otherwise had not been communicated. The magnitude of her role in my life was apparent. For the first time, my appreciation for Denise had been fully expressed.

On a deeper level, I felt the genius of the universe at play. So clearly and precisely, I understood how "hand in hand", through the loving and balancing force of nature, goodness prevailed. As Denise extended her hand in love, she extended love to me, to my family and to the world. In doing so, my parents and I could then extend our hand in love, to the world, to each other and to ourselves.

From the teachings of Abraham and Esther and Jerry Hicks, I have learned that there is no clarity without contrast. In order to see a picture clearly, there must be contrast to define the image. I have learned how to understand the contrast from which my clarity has come. I appreciate the struggles of my childhood and I treasure the wisdom and love that has become mine. I have learned about nature's innate ability to seek balance and goodness. Only the perfection of the universe could deliver such incredible teachers into my life with such different offerings.

I believe that "hand in hand", or one person helping another, lives in every corner of the world. The evidence is never clearer then when natural disasters occur and inspire the most loving acts from mankind. For in all walks of life, the loving and balancing force of nature will bring to each one of us the "godmother" of our lives; a person who offers a loving hand at just the right time, as I found in Denise. We all have the ability to see the goodness in the contrast in which we live and learn. When we are born into this world, we come from the greatest source of goodness—the universe—and life begins through that goodness.

By choosing to see the goodness in all that we live, we can never lose the goodness from that in which we have come!

———✦———

Epilogue
Intrinsic Intelligence

The Genius of All Creation
Is a Part of Who I Am

Within the light of the universe lives the light of all creation. Within the light of our sky lives the light of our world. In light, there is knowledge, communication, and intelligence. In color, there is love, creation, creativity, and greatness.

Radiant light of the sunset sky, how is it that when I stand within your brilliance, I feel as though I stand within my own? When I stand within your intelligence, I feel it as my own. When I stand within your love, I stand knowing my own love within. Magnificent light of the sunset sky, how is it that when I stand within you, I stand knowing the genius of all creation is a part of who I am?

Shimmering light of the starlit skies, how is it that when I look at you, I feel the wonderment of the world that lives within me? How is it that when I look at you, I know the truth of my shining star within? Radiant light of the starlit sky, how is it that when I stand within you, I stand knowing the genius of all creation is a part of who I am?

In light, there is knowledge, there is communication, and there is intelligence. Within the light of the universe lives the light of my spirit.

Since childhood, I have known of my intelligence. It lived quietly within me, confidently, persistently. There was much that I understood, intrinsically, as young as two years old, about people, life, and our universe (within). Yet it was not my time to share. In the presence of others, as a child and into adulthood, my intelligence did not have a voice. It was not seen and was often overlooked, but it always had a home in my heart and within my mind.

For years, I lived with self-doubt and shame that the intelligence that lived within me was somehow not as good, not as respected, as the intelligence that lived within others. And for years, I lived with disappointment and feelings of unworthiness because I was unable to focus in school and therefore was unable to learn traditionally, grammatically, historically, and geographically. I felt that I was not smart.

Ultimately, I discovered differently. While the gap in my education is apparent at times, it does not hold me back. My intrinsic knowing, the intelligence that has always lived within me, which has always been at the foundation of who I truly am, is the genius of my life.

Today, I know that my life's lessons and my schooling have not been typical when compared to most. Yet the teachings of my life are profound. Through the excellence of my life's journey, I have learned that intelligence is much more than a formal education. When I turned the corner in my own life, I learned that the power of a formal education cannot be denied, but I have learned that every form of intelligence has its own time, and every form of life has intelligence. I know that the genius of all creation is a part of who I am and a part of all living matter upon our planet and within our universe. I know that seeing intelligence in all of life's diversity is to also recognize the excellence in all of life's creation.

As my life unfolded, it gradually became clear that this intrinsic knowing, this intelligence that has always lived within me, which I have always wanted to share with the world, needed to ripen, grow, and mature so that it could serve a bigger purpose someday. For me, it was necessary to wait for this intrinsic knowing and form of intelligence to birth into its fullest form, so that one day my knowing could be yours. I now understand that intelligence intrinsically lives within each of us;

with maturity, it will guide us to our greatest life, just as a caterpillar demonstrates so magnificently when it's time to (butter) fly.

To honor our intelligence within, therefore, is to honor the perfection of its presence. As the late poet and peacemaker Mattie Stepanek demonstrated during his brief, yet brilliant, thirteen years of life, intelligence is not always the product of time and maturity. Rather, it is our individual capacity to express the divine and the intrinsic intelligence of our universe.

As I consider the main concerns of our world today, such as healthcare, financial stability, and quality of life, I know that it is the responsibility of each and every one of us to create from within the success that we seek, physically, financially, and emotionally. In doing so, we are then able to contribute to the overall success of our nation, our world, and to our collective cause because it must live within us first.

More and more, we ask our government to be accountable, to be transparent in its actions, so that we may regain our trust in its intentions for our country. As a nation, we have grown. We have evolved through time. We expect excellence because we have stood for excellence, as a nation and throughout the world, for so long. Yet, as trust in our government has waned, so has our excellence.

Often we forget that the government we elect has a direct relationship to the people it serves, just as our personal relationships directly affect the person who lives within each of us. Individually, we must first be accountable and transparent to ourselves and to others so that the trust and excellence we seek in our government will innately live in each and every one of us. When it does, we will see in the government that we elect the leader who lives within each one of us. A new level of excellence will then be at hand, for our nation and our world, in healthcare, finances, and the quality of our lives.

As I consider my relationships with others—and my physical, emotional, and spiritual health—I know that all manifestations of my existence are mere evidence of accepting my genius within. As my life aligns with the person who I came here to be, with the passions of my heart, and with the creativity of my mind, all aspects of my life flourish.

I have learned, emphatically, from the teachings of Abraham and Jerry and Esther Hicks, that when feeling good is our predominant intent, no matter what the circumstance, by utilizing our emotional guidance system to choose the best feeling in *all* of life's situations, we are then in alignment with the source within. For it is in the best feeling or thought that humans are able to access, to know organically, the energy stream where all creation and goodness reside.

When we deliberately invite this creative energy stream into our lives by being positively selective with our thoughts, we are able to deliberately live our best-feeling life. When we argue for our greatness, rather than arguing for our limitations, we manifest the greatness within us, the greatness of our lives.

As I have practiced physical therapy for many years, I have experienced the capacity of our human physical intelligence and the capacity of our innate intelligence to heal and to restore the body from injury and illness.

As I have witnessed both personally and professionally, it is only when the body's environment is conducive to healing that we are able to fully see the evidence of our physical, innate intelligence. To create an environment that is conducive for healing is important, but to create an environment that is conducive for thriving is the key—and that is what seems to have been lost for so many.

As our lifestyles have become more chaotic, so have the environments in which our bodies exist. I often encounter patients who unknowingly discard or ignore the intelligent communication of their bodies as their lives demand countless, unrelenting hours of coming and going from work, family, or friends. More times than not, patients would come for therapy stating that they have lived with the pain and/or physical limitations for months or years, until finally, they couldn't ignore the symptoms, the communication of their body. No longer could they ignore the environment in which they were living. Homeostasis must be restored or the systems will eventually fail.

To allow our genius within is to allow full communication with all aspects of our existence, physically and holistically. This is the medicine we seek. In nature where serenity exists, so lives the beauty of our world. In nature, where chaos exists, as in wildfires, tornadoes, and hurricanes, so live death and destruction. Similarly, just as we find in trees, birds, insects, and animals, when illness or injury is present, the species' innate intelligence guides the animal to rest and recovery. Innately, species of nature know that rest allows the system to heal, and rest allows the cells of the system to communicate with one another in order to do the work in which they know. And in this way, wellness prevails.

As a society, we have forgotten how to rest and how to listen. Through meditation and quiet time, we can find or reconnect with our intelligence within, with the body's communication and with the healing that we seek. As a society, we have been taught to look to external sources for healing, such as seeking treatment from medical practitioners when illness or injury is present. And yes, seeking the care of a medical professional is key. However, if we are to listen first, if we quiet the self and pay attention to the body's communication, illness or injury will have less of a chance to be present.

It wasn't until I received further training and credentialing in the system known as Mechanical Diagnosis and Therapy, or MDT, from the McKenzie Institute International in Raumati Beach, New Zealand, that I awakened to the true power of alignment in the physical and holistic realms and the role of the patient in long-term healing.

Approximately six years ago, I witnessed the sudden release of symptoms for a patient who had been experiencing persistent low back pain for ten years. By utilizing the McKenzie system, where patient self-correction is emphasized, my patient was able to stop the pain. Rarely does a patient remain free of pain after one corrective treatment. It is not until the patient accepts the responsibility to continuously realign within, or to continuously correct the physical misalignment, that there will be long-term recovery. Just as is found through the practice of meditation, it is in repetitive practice that alignment is restored and maintained.

When we align within, physically, mentally, emotionally, and spiritually, we are able to find the space where all systems may communicate and thrive. We are able to discover and become the healers and teachers necessary for our greatest lives to unfold. A healer intrinsically allows. A teacher intrinsically knows. As we align, we intrinsically allow all that we know.

The healer and teacher take flight, embodied as one. Inwardly aligned, the totality of our energy has merged. We are one with the energy of the universe. Physically, we are strong and powerful. We stand tall and mighty like the trees of the forest. We are rich in our color. Our physiques are well maintained with rest, nutrition, activity, consistent, positive thought, and daily meditation. The physical threshold of our bodies is great. Physical illness is rare. Yet this threshold is respected, not pushed past its limit, and allowed restoration when depleted.

The negative impact of stress is minimized through life choices in work and play. The energy of the universe flows through us, unobstructed, as the genius of the human body, the healer, is recognized, permitted, and cherished. We do not fear pain. We seek its knowledge.

This language of the body is respected and welcomed. The teacher knows the medium-ship of this work and the broader scope of this medicine. The healer comes forward when needed, but the teacher knows intrinsically when the body is unable to heal when left to its own resources. Through the perfection of the universe, we are guided to seek the wisdom and expertise of those who know. Ultimately, we return to alignment through life or death.

Mentally, we have clarity and decisiveness. We trust inner guidance. We move forward with confidence in our daily decisions and our interactions with others, and we have integrity and congruency between our thoughts and our actions. We seek knowledge, a nutrient for growth. We embody the power of disciplined focus; it sets us apart from all other living matter on our planet. With our human focus, we have the ability to create the life that we wish to live, personally, professionally, and spiritually. We are empowered through focus. We trust life's path.

Emotionally, we are stable. We know all is well with self, family, society, our country, and our world. We do not seek to change or motivate others in their actions. Rather, we seek to inspire and call forward the excellence that lives within each of us—the excellence of the mind, character, heart, and spirit.

Emotionally, we are independent. We choose happiness, joy, and calm, regardless of our surroundings, in people, places, and events. We are empathetic toward all those in need. We take action to help when inspired from within.

Our spirit takes flight. We are weightless, and we soar. We merge with the intelligence in nature and live in this energy of non-resistance. We are breathless in delight. There are no limits to our existence. We are one with the universe, in thought, feelings, and knowledge. Our energies have united. Our hearts beat as one with the heart of the universe. The creativity of the mind is unleashed, as is the genius that guides our lives. We acknowledge sole responsibility for all that we live. We treat others with respect, unconditionally. And, we stand with humility and appreciation for all that we have been given on our lives' journeys.

Inwardly aligned, our lives are the best they can be. We are radiant beings of love and abundance in our health, our wealth, and our wisdom. We stand powerfully in life as beacons of light demonstrating the evidence of our inner successes.

Our purposes are clear. We have a path. Finally, we are true to our self. We are at peace. We have tranquility. We live knowing that all is well in our (inner) universe. We recognize that the joy we feel internally is greater than any joy we could experience from material possessions. Our joy is eternal.

Index